International Financial Reporting Standards in Depth
Volume 2: Solutions

PUBLISHING

International Financial Reporting Standards in Depth

Volume 2: Solutions

Robert J. Kirk

ELSEVIER
BUTTERWORTH
HEINEMANN

AMSTERDAM • BOSTON • HEIDELBERG • LONDON • NEW YORK • OXFORD
PARIS • SAN DIEGO • SAN FRANCISCO • SINGAPORE • SYDNEY • TOKYO

CIMA Publishing
An Imprint of Elsevier
Linacre House, Jordan Hill, Oxford OX2 8DP
30 Corporate Drive, Burlington, MA 01803

First published 2005

British Library Cataloguing in Publication Data
A catalogue record for this book is available from the British Library

Library of Congress Cataloguing in Publication Data Control Number: 2005923930

ISBN 0 7506 64738 (Set)
ISBN 0 7506 67788 (Volume 1)
ISBN 0 7506 67796 (Volume 2)

For information on all Elsevier Butterworth-Heinemann publications
visit our website at http://books.elsevier.com

Typeset by Newgen Imaging Systems Pvt Ltd, Chennai, India
Printed and bound in Great Britain

Working together to grow
libraries in developing countries

www.elsevier.com | www.bookaid.org | www.sabre.org

ELSEVIER   BOOK AID International   Sabre Foundation

Contents

The regulatory framework and the standard-setting process – solutions

Solution 1.1: Vincible

(a) In accordance with IAS:

(i) Income statement for the year ended 30 September 2002

		$000
Sales revenue (473,300 T/B + 18,000 joint venture)		491,300
Cost of sales	(W2)	366,000
Gross profit		125,300
Operating expenses (per T/B)		18,400
Impairment of non current asset (development costs 75,000 − 15,000 amortised = 60,000 − 40,000 net realisable value = 20,000)	(W3)	20,000
Profit on the ordinary activities before interest		86,900
Loan interest (5,000 paid +5,000 due)		10,000
Profit before tax		76,900
Taxation (15,000 current − 1,100 deferred tax)		13,900
Net profit from ordinary activities for the period		63,000

(ii) Statement of changes in equity for the year ended 30 September 2002

	Ordinary shares $000	Revaluation reserve $000	Accumulated profits $000	Total $000
Balance at 1 October 2001	100,000	nil	13,300	113,300
Revaluation surplus on leasehold property (W5)		126,000		126,000
Transfer to deferred tax (W4)		(7,200)		(7,200)
Transfer to realised reserves re leasehold property ((126,000 surplus − 7,200 tax)/ 18 years left)		(6,600)	6,600	
Net profit for the period (63,000 − 24,000 proposed dividend)			39,000	39,000
Proposed dividend (400,000 25c shares × 6c)			24,000	24,000
Dividends paid			(15,500)	(15,500)
	100,000	112,200	67,400	279,600

(iii) Balance sheet as at 30 September 2002

	$000	$000
Non-current assets		
Development expenditure ($40m/4yrs = $10m net $30m)		30,000
Property, plant and equipment (*W5*)		368,300
		398,300
Current assets		
Inventory (37,700 + 2,500 joint venture)	40,200	
Trade receivables (49,200 + 3,500 joint venture)	52,700	
Bank (per T/B)	12,100	
		105,000
Total assets		503,300
Total equity and liabilities		
Ordinary shares of 25c each		100,000
Reserves		
Accumulated profits	67,400	
Revaluation reserve	112,200	
		179,600
		279,600
Non-current liabilities		
10% Convertible loan stock	100,000	
Deferred tax (70,000 × 25%)	17,500	
		117,500
Current liabilities (82,200 per T/B + 4,000 joint venture + 5,000 interest due + 15,000 current tax)		106,200
		503,300

(b) Earnings per share

Basic

Earnings attributable to ordinary shares	$63 million
Number of shares in issue (100 million × 25c)	400 million
Earnings per share	15.8 cents

Diluted

Earnings	$70.5m
Number of shares	480m
Earnings per share	14.7 cents

Ranking of dilution:

	Increase in earnings ($)	Increase in shares	Incremental earnings
Director's options	Nil	20 (50 × $1.60/$4)	$ Nil[1]
Convertible shares	7.5m ($10m × 75% net of tax)	60	0.125[2]

Calculation of diluted earnings per share:

Basic earnings	$63m	400m	15.8c
Options[1]	Nil	20	
	63m	420m	15.0c
Convertible shares[2]	7.5m	60m	
Diluted	70.5m	480m	14.7c

Under IAS 33 *Earnings Per Share*, potential ordinary shares should be treated as dilutive when their conversion would decrease earnings per share from continuing operations. Where there is more than one class of dilutive securities, as above, IAS 33 requires them to be ranked in the order of the most dilutive to the least dilutive.

Working

W1   Joint ventures
Under IAS 31 *Financial Reporting of Joint Ventures*, each venturer in jointly controlled operations must account for the assets it controls and the liabilities it incurs in its balance sheet and the expenses/incomes in its income statement. As this is not a separate entity, the above should be included in the appropriate 'line' items in the financial statements – e.g. share of sales in turnover etc.

W2   Cost of sales

	$000
Opening inventory	27,500
Purchases	310,500
Joint venture – cost of sales	8,000
Depreciation: – leasehold property (270,000/18 yrs)	15,000
– plant (124,800 − 48,800 × 20%)	15,200
– plant joint venture (70,000/4 yrs)	17,500
– development (40,000/4yrs)	10,000
Closing inventory	(37,700)
	366,000

W3   Development expenditure
There is an impairment and the asset must be written down from its book value of $60m ($75 less accumulated amortisation $15m) to its recoverable amount, i.e. the higher of NRV ($40m) and value in use ($30m), resulting in an impairment of $60m − 40m = $20m.

W4   Deferred taxation
The timing difference between the tax base and carrying value of fixed assets of $70m should be provided at 25%, leaving a closing liability of $17.5m. However, $7.2m of this ($28.8m × 25%) belongs to revaluation reserve, leaving a balance of $10.3m. As the opening provision was $11.4m, there is a need to reduce the liability and release tax of $1.1m to the income statement.

W5 Non-current assets

	$
Leasehold property:	
Cost	200,000
Depreciation at 1 October 2001 (7 yrs, i.e. $56,000/8,000)	56,000
Net book value prior to revaluation	144,000
Revaluation surplus	126,000
Valuation 1 October 2001	270,000
Depreciation (270,000/18 yrs, i.e. 25 less 7 yrs elapsed)	15,000
Net book value at 30 September 2002	255,000
Plant:	
Cost	124,800
Depreciation (124,800 − 48,800 × 20%) = 15,200	
Net book value (124,800 − 48,800 − 15,200)	60,800
Plant − joint venture cost	70,000
Depreciation (70,000/4 yrs)	17,500
Net book value (70,000 − 17,500)	52,500
Total net book value (255,000 + 60,800 + 52,500)	368,300

Solution 1.2: Stilson (ACCA Accounting and Audit Practice)

Income statement of Stilson for the year ended 31 March 2001

	$000	$000
Sales revenue (26,750 per T/B + 3,000) (*W4*)		29,750
Cost of sales (*W1*)		(19,026)
Gross profit		10,724
Operating expenses (1,340 per T/B + 1,250 property rent per T/B)		(2,590)
Other operating income (per T/B profit on sale of property)		3,400
Financing cost (200 paid + 200 accrued)		(400)
Profit before tax		11,134
Taxation		(2,400)
Net profit from ordinary activities for the period		8,734

Statement of changes in equity for the year ended 31 March 2001

	Share capital	Revaluation reserve	Accumulated profits	Total
	$000	$000	$000	$000
Balance at 31 March 2000	5,000	nil	580	5,580
Surplus on revaluation of property (*W2*)		5,200		5,200
Net profit for the period			8,734	8,734
Dividends (2m interim + 5m × 4 × 15c final)			(5,000)	(5,000)
Transfer to realised profits		(280)	280	−
Balance at 31 March 2001	5,000	4,920	4,594	14,514

Balance sheet as at 31 March 2001

	$000	$000
Assets		
Property, plant and equipment (W3)		12,584
Current assets		
Inventory	2,800	
Amounts due from construction contracts (W4)	1,100	
Trade receivables	8,620	
Cash	4,180	16,700
Total assets		29,284
Equity and liabilities		
Capital and reserves:		
Equity shares of 25c each		5,000
Reserves:		
Revaluation reserve (5,200 − 280) (W2)	4,920	
Accumulated profits (see above)	4,594	9,514
		14,514
Non-current liabilities		
8% Loan note	5,000	
Provision for voucher scheme (W1)	630	5,630
Current liabilities		
Trade payables	3,540	
Accrued loan interest	200	
Income taxes	2,400	
Proposed dividends	3,000	9,140
Total equity and liabilities		29,284

Notes to the financial statements:

1. Sales revenue includes $3m attributable to long-term construction contracts, and cost of sales includes $1.8m attributable to long-term construction contracts.
2. Other operating income relates to the profit on disposal of one of the company's properties.

Working

W1 Cost of sales

			$000	$000
Opening inventory				1,900
Purchases				16,000
Provision for voucher scheme				*630
Construction contract costs	(W4)			1,800
Depreciation: – buildings	($9m/15 years)		600	
plant	(20% × 4,480)		896	1,496
Closing inventory				(2,800)
				19,026

*Voucher scheme $3m × 50% (est. redempt.) × 70% (less 30% margin) × 60% (discounted). This is likely to be deducted from sales in the future, if material.

W2   Depreciation: buildings

- Depreciation of buildings before revaluation ($8m/25 years) = $320,000
- Accumulated depreciation at 31 March 2000 ($3.2m/$320,000) = 10 years
- Revalued asset should be depreciated over remaining 15 years (i.e. $9m/15 years) = $600,000
- Revaluation surplus $5.2m ($12m − ($10m − $3.2m)) = $5.2m ($1m relates to land and $4.2m to buildings)
- Surplus on buildings should be released to accumulated profits as it is realised in line with future depreciation. The transfer for this year should be $4.2m/15 years = $280,000.

W3   Property, plant and equipment

	$000	$000
Land and buildings at valuation	12,000	
Depreciation (*W2*)	(600)	11,400
Plant at cost	4,480	
Depreciation (2,400 + 896)	(3,296)	1,184
		12,584

W4   Construction contract

Contract is 30% complete ($3m/$10m × 100)

	$000
Total profit ($10m − $6m)	4,000
Attributable profit (30% × $4m)	1,200
Contract revenue (work certified)	3,000
Contract cost of sales ($3m revenue − $1.2m profit)	1,800
Amount due from customers	
(1,900 costs to date + 1,200 profit − progress billings 2,000)	1,100

Solution 1.3: S

(a)   Explanation of accounting concept of substance over form

The accounting concept of substance over form is covered in IAS 1 *Presentation of Financial Statements*. Substance over form effectively means that accountants must always report the commercial reality of transactions rather than their legal form if the two come into conflict. The preparer of financial statements must get behind the legal veil and examine what is really going on in commercial terms in a transaction. If the substance differs from the legal form, then IAS 1 requires the substance of the transaction to be adopted in the financial statements. In order to establish substance, it may be necessary to investigate a whole series of transactions together rather than individually – e.g. sale and repurchase arrangement – to see whether or not a genuine sale has actually taken place. One of the keystones in the decision as to whether substance effects form is making the decision as to whether or not the transaction has a material effect on the risks and rewards of ownership.

An example of substance in practice can be found in IAS 17 *Leases*, which effectively forces lessees to record finance leases on their balance sheet as all the risks and rewards of ownership have been transferred to them by the lessor. It is effectively the same accounting treatment as if the asset had always been owned by the company.

(b)   Treatment of transactions

Sale and leaseback

The land and buildings were sold at a price which was well below the current book value – $50m instead of $80m. This would imply that it was not an arm's length transaction. The repurchase price has also been set in terms of the original selling price plus interest, rather than at market value at the time of the repurchase. As interest is to be charged from the original date of sale, this implies that there is an expectation that the asset will be re-purchased and this is supported by the annual rental which, at 15% (($7.5m/$50m) × 100) of the purchase price, seems artificially high.

Taking both transactions together, it is clear that the substance of the arrangement would appear to be a financing one with S effectively raising funds against the security of the property. S is almost certain to repurchase the property in due course, as $50m plus interest will be significantly less than the current value of $80m plus any future inflation.

S should clearly treat the transaction as a financing arrangement, thus keeping the property on the balance sheet and also reflecting the cash received as a liability. The annual interest should be charged to the income statement and the corresponding credit entry added to the liability. Ultimately when it is repurchased any cash payment should eliminate the original loan plus interest accrued.

The journal entries required to correct the situation are as follows:

	Debit	**Credit**
Non-current assets – land and buildings	$80m	
Loss on disposal (income statement)		$30m
Loan (included in non-current liabilities)		$50m

In addition, the annual interest will need to be charged to income each year at the current rate plus 5%, and the corresponding credit added to the loan.

Sale on consignment

In deciding whether or not a sale has taken place, it is essential to determine which party has the risks and rewards of ownership. Taking each of the points in turn:

- S must pay 50% on delivery and the balance when the cars are sold. If prices change prior to the sale date, S still pays the same amount to its supplier. They therefore bear the risks and earn the rewards on those price changes.
- If cars remain unsold after 3 months, S has to pay an administration charge of 20% – which also suggests that they have taken up the risks and rewards of ownership.

From the information provided, on balance, it would appear that the inventory should be recorded in the books of S despite the fact that they do not have legal title. The journal entries required to correct the position are as follows:

	Debit	Credit
Closing inventory (included on balance sheet)	$6m	
Cost of sales (included in income statement)		$6m
Purchases	$6m	
Pre-payments (monies paid to date)		$3m
Trade payables		$3m

Finance lease

The decision must be made as to whether or not, in substance, this can be recorded as a finance or as an operating lease in the books of S. There are three factors which suggest that it should be treated as a finance lease:

- The useful life of the asset is 5–7 years and the lease term only 6 years, thus suggesting that S has use of the asset over substantially all of the asset's life.
- The fair value of the equipment is $7,650,296, which equates to the present value of the asset discounted at the implicit rate of interest in the lease of 7%.
- S has agreed to insure and maintain the equipment, thus retaining all the substantial risks pertaining to the asset.

All of these factors indicate that S has retained all the substantial risks and rewards of ownership and should therefore record both the asset and its related liability on the balance sheet under IAS 17 *Leases*. The asset would be included within property etc. in the non-current asset section of the balance sheet and the loan within non-current liabilities.

The finance lease payments and interest are shown below:

Year	Opening balance $	Payments $	$	Interest for year (7%) $	Closing balance $
1	7,650,296 (given)	(1,500,000)	6,150,296	430,521	6,580,817
2	6,580,817	(1,500,000)	5,080,817	355,657	5,436,474
3	5,436,474	(1,500,000)	3,936,474	275,553	4,212,027
4	4,212,027	(1,500,000)	2,712,027	189,842	2,901,869
5	2,901,869	(1,500,000)	1,401,869	98,131	1,500,000
6	1,500,000	(1,500,000)			
		(9,000,000)		1,349,704	

T accounts

Finance lease obligations:

Bank	1,500,000	Balance – capital	7,650,296
Balance c/d	7,500,000	Balance – interest in suspense	1,349,704
	1,500,000		9,000,000
		Balance b/d	7,500,000

Finance interest in suspense:

Balance	1,349,704	Finance cost (income statement)	430,521
		Balance c/d	919,183
	1,349,704		1,349,704
Balance b/d	919,183		

Balance sheet extract

	Total	Current liability	Non-current liability
	$	**$**	**$**
Total repayments	7,500,000	1,500,000	6,000,000
Interest in suspense	919,183	430,521	919,183
	6,580,817	1,069,429	5,080,817
		+ 430,521 accrued interest	
		1,500,000	

2

Asset valuation: accounting for tangible fixed assets – solutions

Solution 2.1: Broadoak

(a) Measuring the cost of tangible non-current assets, and capitalising subsequent expenditure

(i) How the initial cost of tangible non-current assets should be measured

Although the broad principles of accounting for non-current assets are well understood by the accounting profession, applying these principles to practical situations has resulted in complications and inconsistency. For the most part, IAS 16 *Property, Plant and Equipment* codifies existing good practice, but it does include specific rules which are intended to achieve improved consistency and more transparency.

IAS 16 requires property, plant and equipment to be initially recorded at cost. The cost of an item of property, plant and equipment comprises its purchase price and any other costs directly attributable to bringing the asset into a working condition for its intended use. This can consist as follows:

- The purchase price, which is calculated after the deduction of any trade discounts or rebates (but not early settlement discounts), but it does include any transport and handling costs (delivery, packing and insurance), non-refundable taxes (e.g. sale taxes such as VAT, stamp duty, import duty). If the payment is deferred beyond normal credit terms, this should be taken into account either by the use of discounting or substituting a cash equivalent price.
- Directly attributable costs, which are the incremental costs that would have been avoided had the assets not been acquired. For self constructed assets, this includes the labour costs of own employees. Abnormal costs such as wastage and errors are specifically excluded.
- Installation costs, site preparation costs, and professional fees (legal fees, architect's fees, however, are permitted).

In addition to the 'traditional' costs above, two further groups of cost may be capitalised. IAS 23 *Borrowing Costs* permits (under the allowed alternative method) directly attributable borrowing costs to be capitalised as part of the asset. Also IAS 37 *Provisions,*

Contingent Liabilities and Contingent Assets states that if the estimated costs of removing and dismantling an asset and restoring its site qualify as a liability, they should be provided for and added to the cost of the relevant asset. This happens in cases of decommissioning a nuclear plant or oilfield. Finally, the carrying amount of an asset may be reduced by any applicable government grants under IAS 20 *Accounting for Government Grants and Disclosure of Government Assistance*, although the deferred income approach is more popular in practice.

(ii)   Subsequent expenditure

The appropriate accounting treatment of subsequent expenditure on non-current assets depended upon whether or not it represented a revenue expense, in effect maintenance or a repair, or whether it represented an improvement that should be capitalised. IAS 16 bases the question of capitalisation of subsequent expenditure on whether it results in a probable future economic benefit in excess of the amount originally assessed for the asset. All other subsequent expenditure should be recognised in the income statement as it is incurred. Examples of circumstances where subsequent expenditure should be capitalised are where it:

- modifies the asset to enhance its future economic benefits;
- upgrades an asset to improve the quality of performance;
- is on a new production process that reduces operating costs.

IAS 16 also permits component accounting. Where a large asset such as a ship or aircraft is broken down into smaller components and these are depreciated over their individual shorter lives, then any expenditure incurred subsequently to overhaul those assets may be capitalised as the original asset has already been fully depreciated. However, normal servicing and overhaul expenditure is written off immediately.

(b)   Revaluation of non-current assets and the accounting treatment of surpluses/deficits on revaluation

Under IAS 16, revaluations are permitted under its allowed alternative treatment rules for the measurement of assets subsequent to their initial recognition. The standard attempts to bring some order and consistency to the practice of revaluations.

Where an entity chooses to revalue a tangible non-current asset, it must also revalue the entire class of assets to which it belongs. Further, sufficiently regular revaluations should be made such that the carrying amounts of revalued assets should not differ materially to their fair values at the balance sheet date. The standard stops short of requiring annual valuations, but it does contain detailed rules on the basis and frequency of valuation. It should be noted that where an asset has been written down to its recoverable amount due to impairment, this is not classed as being a policy of revaluation. The effect of the above is that it prevents selective or favourable valuations being reported whilst ignoring adverse movements, and where a company has chosen to revalue its assets (or class thereof), the values must be kept up to date.

Surpluses/deficits

These are measured as the difference between the revalued amounts and the book (carrying) values at the date of the valuation.

Increases (gains) are taken to equity under revaluation reserves (via a Statement of changes in equity) unless they reverse a previous loss (on the same asset) that has been charged to the income statement – in which case they should be recognised as income.

Decreases in valuations (revaluation losses) should normally be charged to the income statement. However, where they relate to an asset that has previously been revalued upwards, then to the extent that the losses do not exceed the amount standing to the credit of the asset in the revaluation reserve, they should be charged directly to that reserve.

Any impairment loss on revalued property, plant and equipment, recognisable under IAS 36 *Impairment of Assets*, is treated as a revaluation loss under IAS 16.

Gains and losses on disposal

Gains or losses on disposal are measured as the difference between the net sale proceeds and the carrying value of assets at the date of sale. In the past some companies reverted to historic cost values to calculate a gain on disposal, thus inflating the gain (assuming assets had increased in value). All gains and losses should be recognised in the income statement in the period of the disposal. Any revaluation surplus standing to the credit of a disposed asset should be transferred to accumulated realised profits (as a movement on reserves).

(c)   The initial cost of plant – Broadoak

	$	$
Basic list price of plant		240,000
Less trade discount of 12.5% on list price		(30,000)
		210,000
Shipping handling and installation costs		2,750
Estimated pre-production testing		12,500
Maintenance contract (not permitted)		
Site preparation costs (normal only)		
– electrical cable installation (14,000 − 6,000)	8,000	
– concrete reinforcement	4,500	
– own labour costs	7,500	20,000
Dismantling costs and restoration costs (15,000 + 3,000)		18,000
Initial cost of plant		263,250

Note: The early settlement discount is a revenue item and IAS 16 expressly disallows it from being capitalised. The maintenance cost is also a revenue item, although a proportion of it would be a pre-payment at the end of the year of acquisition (the amount would be dependent on the date on acquisition).

The cost of the specification error must be charged to the income statement.

(d) Leasehold property – extracts from financial statements

Income statement			*Balance sheet*		
Amortisation	$20,000	(2000)	Leasehold property	$231,000	(2000)
	21,000	(2001)		175,000	(2001)

Change in equity statement					
Revaluation loss	25,000	(2001)	*Revaluation reserve*		
			Revaluation reserve	$0,000	1.10.99
			Revaluation surplus	11,000	(2000)
				61,000	
			Transfer to acc. profits	1,000	$(1/11 \times 11,000)$
				60,000	
			Revaluation loss	10,000	
				50,000	(2001)

Working

	$
Cost 1 October 1999	240,000
Amortisation to 30.9.2000 (240,000/12 years)	(20,000)
	220,000
Revaluation gain	11,000
Revised carrying value at 30 September 2000	231,000
Amortisation 2001 (231,000/11 years)	(21,000)
	210,000
Revaluation loss (direct to reserves) (11,000 − 1,000)	(10,000)
Remaining loss to income statement	(25,000)
Revised carrying value at 30 September 2001	175,000

Solution 2.2: L

(a) Why IAS 16 requires revaluation of assets in relevant classes, and why these should be up to date

IAS 16 permits a choice between revaluation or not of property, plant etc. If a company opts for revaluation, then the standard's objective is to ensure that the values reflect up-to-date fair values at the balance sheet date. That is to ensure consistency, which is one of the main qualitative characteristics in the IASB's Framework.

To ensure both consistency and comparability, revaluation must be applied consistently to all assets in that class. This ensures that a company's directors cannot 'cherry pick' the assets which are rising in value and ignore those that are falling.

Again to ensure consistency, IAS 16 requires that the valuations be kept up to date, at fair value. This does not require an annual valuation, but they should be carried out with sufficient regularity to ensure that the carrying value does not differ materially from the fair value at each balance sheet date. Market value is the normal valuation, but depreciated replacement cost should be adopted where there is no evidence of market values.

(b) Is it logical to permit both cost and valuation methods?

In line with several other IASs, there is both a benchmark (cost) and an allowed alternative (valuation). The rationale is the lack of any agreed consensus as to what the correct approach should be, with the USA being totally opposed to valuation and the UK and others being largely in favour of at least valuing properties. It is up to individual preparers to weigh up the cost and benefits of revaluation. It is not logical to offer both alternatives, but hopefully the revaluation group of standard setters which is currently meeting will come up with firm proposals that will arrive at a consensus approach to the issue. That may, however, be several years hence.

(c) Calculation of property values

Property should appear on the balance sheet as follows:

	$m
Factory A	160
Factory B	120
Factory C	40
	320

The revaluation gain/loss should be calculated as follows:

Factory A

Depreciation per T/B	70
Current year charge (250 cost × 2%)	5
	75
Cost	250
Net book value	175
Valuation	160
Loss on revaluation	15

There is no revaluation reserve to offset this loss, so it must be charged to the income statement.

Factory B

Depreciation per T/B	60
Current year charge (150 cost × 2%)	3
	63
Cost	150
Net book value	87
Valuation	120
Gain on revaluation	33

This gain should be credited to equity and also be recorded in the Statement of changes in equity.

Factory C

Depreciation from T/B	48
Current year charge (134 × 2%)	3
	51
Cost	134
Net book value	83
Valuation	40
Loss on revaluation	43

As this factory was never previously revalued, the loss cannot be offset against a previous revaluation surplus and the loss must go direct to income.

(d)   Impact of revaluation on key accounting ratios

The two main accounting ratios affected by revaluation are return on capital employed (ROCE) and the gearing ratio.

ROCE

This is calculated as a percentage of net profit to capital employed. If fixed assets are revalued, then the depreciation must also be increased in line with the revaluation.

An upwards revaluation will therefore result in a decrease in return and an increase in capital employed, and thus a double 'whammy' on the calculation of ROCE. This will result in a fall in the return on capital employed.

Overall in L's case, however, there is a downward revaluation, thus improving both return and reducing capital employed, resulting in an increase in ROCE.

Gearing ratio

This is the percentage of long-term debt to shareholders' funds plus long-term debt. If the revaluation is upwards the gearing ratio will drop as the bottom line is increased, but there is no adjustment to the top line. If revaluation is downwards, the reverse will happen.

Overall impact

The position of both ratios will have opposite effects. Profitability will appear to go down as ROCE falls, but conversely the gearing ratio will be improved, enabling the company possibly to borrow further monies based on the strength of their assets.

Solution 2.3: K

(a) Initial cost of oven permitted under IAS 16

	£
List price	50,000
Wages and materials pre production	800
Costs of disposal	16,000
Total cost	66,800

All costs are permitted under IAS 16 to get the asset to its intended location and working condition. That will enable the wages and materials associated with testing and calibrating the oven prior to production to be incorporated, but not those since the start of operations.

The inclusion of the expected costs of disposal is more difficult. It has been included above on the grounds that the cost of acquiring the oven must also include the costs of disposal, as the government has enforced the cost to be cleaned up at the end and specially disposed. That is in line with IAS 37 *Provisions, Contingent Liabilities and Contingent Assets*, when decommissioning costs should be reported as both an asset and liability at the time an oilfield or nuclear plant is created. A different view might exclude the costs entirely and only record them as expenses when incurred.

(b) Historic cost and valuation bases

Calculation of historic cost and valuation bases for oven at the end of the first year

Historic cost:

	£
Profit and loss extract	
Depreciation (£66,800/expected useful life of 5 years)	13,360
Balance sheet extract	
Cost	66,800
Less accumulated depreciation to date	13,360
Net book value	53,440

Valuation:

	£
Profit and loss extract	
Impairment loss (£66,800 − £28,000 recoverable amount)	38,800
Balance sheet extract	
Valuation	28,000

Discussion of the relevance and reliability of both sets of figures

Historic costs are reliable in that there is a clear audit trail to identify their actual costs. The figures are generally reliable. However, there are still subjective judgements to be made *re* choice of economic life and ultimate disposal scrap value. The figures are not relevant as the book value does not represent the current value of the asset, particularly in this case.

The valuation model is more relevant than historic cost, as it represents the current market value of the asset provided it is based upon actual market transactions. However, it is often the case that no market exists for second-hand specialised assets, and this leads to very subjective and possibly erroneous valuations. However, current values are more useful for making decisions, even if they are less reliable than historic costs.

Solution 2.4: Aztech

(a) Why the requirements of both IAS 16 and IAS 37 need to be investigated as well as IAS 16 when accounting for tangible non-current assets

Circumstances may arise where subsequent to initial recognition, the book value of a tangible non-current asset may not be economically recoverable from future business activity. Although future production may be possible, this may be insufficient to recover the current book value in the future. IAS 36 *Impairment of Assets* requires a write down of the book value of an asset to its recoverable amount, and the reduction charged as an immediate expense in the income statement. If it reverses a previous revaluation uplift, it should be charged directly against the revaluation surplus (per IAS 16 *Property, Plant and Equipment*). Thus the two standards need to be consulted in this area, as any impairment loss of a revalued asset requires consideration of the determination of whether the asset is impaired (IAS 36) and how this loss is going to be dealt with if the asset has been revalued. In addition, IAS 36 deals with the depreciation charge for an impaired asset and the reversal of an impairment loss of an asset. Again, in this latter case if the asset has been revalued, both IAS 16 and IAS 36 need consulting.

After the initial recognition of an asset, an enterprise may incur further expenditure on that asset. IAS 37 *Provisions, Contingent Liabilities and Contingent Assets* has stated that periodic maintenance costs cannot be accrued in advance of a shut down, and decommissioning costs and other environmental costs relating to an asset must be recognised as soon as there is an obligating event. These costs cannot be built up over the life of an asset but must be provided for in full when the obligating event occurs. IAS 37 deals with the measurement and recognition of the provision (i.e. the credit entry), and IAS 16 deals with the accounting for the debit entry resulting in a smooth interaction between the two statements.

(b) Accounting for hotels and whether or not current depreciation policy is acceptable

Valuation of hotels on balance sheet

IAS 16 states that on the revaluation of land and buildings, they should usually be valued on the basis of their market values. Properties retired from use should be valued on the basis of their carrying amount at the date of retirement subject to an annual impairment review. Thus on 31 March 2000, the hotels will be valued as follows:

	$m	$m
Open market value	19	
Less property to be sold	(2.5)	
		16.5
Property surplus to requirements (carrying value)	3	
Impaired value – lower of carrying value and recoverable amount ($3m compared with the higher of $2m and $(2.5 − 0.2)m		2.3
Balance sheet value		18.8

Under IFRS 5 *Non-Current Assets Held For Sale and the Presentation of Discontinued Operations*, any non-current asset which fulfils six criteria must be transferred to current assets at their recoverable amount, with a loss of £3m − 2.3m = £0.7m being charged to income.

Policy of non-depreciation

A policy of non-depreciation cannot be permitted merely on the grounds of high maintenance. The latter may increase the life of the asset, but not its residual value at the end of its useful life. It is also argued that depreciation results in matching the expense against the revenue generated by the asset; it is not a valuation of that asset. The only assets that can strictly avoid depreciation are investment properties and land. The policy is currently therefore unacceptable, but the revised standard, IAS 16, may well reintroduce it as it enables entities to revalue residual values at the end of each accounting year, not just at the date of acquisition of the asset.

(c)   Accounting for the aircraft fleet

(i)   At 31 March 2000

	$000
Cost of manufacturing the aircraft	28,000
Capitalisation of borrowing costs ($20m × 10% + $22m × 10% × 3/4 yr)	3,650
	31,650

Capitalisation is only permitted during construction and should stop when the asset is substantially ready for operations – thus 1 January 2000 and not 31 March 2000 would appear to be the deadline under IAS 23 *Borrowing Costs*.

Under IAS 36 *Impairment of Assets*, if a constructed asset is valued at more than its recoverable amount it must be written down to that figure. That is currently $30m (net selling price), which is $1m greater than its current use value.

(ii)   At 31 March 2001

	$000
Engines (30% × 30,000 = 9,000/3 yrs = 3,000 depreciation)	6,000
Body parts (70% × 30,000 = 21,000/8 yrs = 2,625 depreciation)	18,375
	24,375

Revaluation loss (to income statement)	(3,375)
Closing book value	21,000

Loss is split:

6,000/24,375 × 3,375 = 831, i.e. 6,000 − 831	5,169
18,375/24,375 × 3,375 = 2,544, i.e. 18,375 − 2,544	15,831
	21,000

At 31 March 2002:

	$000
Engines (5,169/2 yrs = 2,585 depreciation)	2,584
Body parts (15,831/7 yrs = 2,262 depreciation)	13,569
	16,153
Revaluation gain (to income statement)	3,375
Revaluation reserve	72
Closing book value	19,600

Where an asset's carrying amount is increased due to revaluation, the increase should be credited to equity. However, if it reverses a previous write down to income by the same asset, the amount written down should be reversed and only any excess credited to revaluation reserves and equity.

Engines (9,000 + 30% × 72 = 9,022 − 5,585 depreciation)	3,437
Body parts (21,000 + 70% × 72 = 21,050 − 4,887 depreciation)	16,163
	19,600

(iii)   At 31 March 2003

	$000
Engines (3,437/1 yr = 3,437 depreciation)	nil
Body parts (16,163/6 yrs = 2,694 depreciation)	13,469
	13,469
Replacement engines	15,000
Closing book value	28,469

Solution 2.5: Low Paints

(a)   Has the calculation of earnings per share been correctly calculated?

Earnings per share (EPS) is prescribed by IAS 33 *Earnings per Share*. The numerator in the calculation is the net profit attributable to ordinary shareholders, and that has been calculated in accordance with other prescribed accounting standards. It is possible still for directors to choose between several legitimate accounting policies in order to boost earnings, as they may impact on the ultimate bonus paid to directors. The denominator is the weighted average number of ordinary shares outstanding during the period, but this is tightly controlled by IAS 33.

There are a number of events outlined in the case of Low Paints that could have affected the calculation of earnings per share:

(i) IAS 20 *Accounting for Government Grants and Disclosure of Government Assistance* permits two methods of accounting for the grant, either:
   • setting the grant off against the cost of the asset and depreciating the net figure; or
   • recording the grant within deferred income and releasing it to income over the life of the asset to offset the depreciation charge.
   The grant must therefore be taken out of income, leaving only $500,000 ($5m/10 years) to be credited to income. The balance of $4.5m should be recorded as deferred income or deducted from the cost of the asset.
   There is a recent DP coming from New Zealand recommending immediate credit to income, but that cannot be used to override an existing standard. The argument given in that paper is that grants do not meet the definition of a liability, and as such could never be recorded as liabilities on balance sheet.

(ii) The directors have not taken account of the new issue of shares made at the initial public offering. The EPS was calculated using the number of shares in issue when Mr Low retired from the company (6m at $1). The new shares should have been time apportioned, i.e. 1m + 100,000 sponsor's shares, and added to the denominator. The costs of issue are regarded as part of the consideration received and are therefore deducted from equity (as per SIC 17). They should not go to income, but should instead be set off against share premium. The accounting entry should have been:

			$	$
Dr		Share premium	300,000	
	Cr	Cash		180,000
		Share capital		100,000
		Share premium		20,000

(iii) Leases are governed by IAS 17 *Leases*, but the substance of this transaction is that of a secured loan, thus requiring the presentation of the original asset and receipts as a loan. The profit will therefore be eliminated from income and the property depreciated at a rate of 5% on the carrying value of $4m. An interest charge of $250,000, i.e. ($5.5m − $4.5m)/4 years should also be recorded for the implicit interest in the agreement.

(iv) Normally, post-balance sheet events should be ignored in calculating the capital structure for EPS. However, it should be amended for the bonus element in post year-end changes in the number of shares. This is calculated as follows:

Fair value of shares before rights	$2
Theoretical ex rights price	$1.92 (i.e. 4 × $2 = $8 + rights issue 1 × $1.60
	= $9.60/5 shares)
Bonus element	$2/$1.92 (i.e. 25/24)

The revised earnings per share calculations should be as follows:

		$000
Net profit for the year as originally prepared		4,800
(i) government grant	(5,000)	
grant release	500	(4,500)
(ii) cash paid – fee	180	
ordinary shares	(120)	60
(iii) profit on sale eliminated	(500)	
depreciation	(200)	
interest charge	(250)	
		(950)
Adjusted net loss for the year		(590)
Ordinary shares of $1		6m
(i) 1.1m × 10/12		0.917m
(ii) Bonus element (1 for 24)		0.288m
		7.205m
Loss per share		$0.082

(b)   Did the directors act unethically?

The treatment of government grants would appear to indicate that the directors were attempting to boost EPS. They should be aware of the content of IAS 20, and would appear to be finding a way to boost their bonus. Discussion Papers may indicate current thinking, but they are not yet best practice.

It is more likely that the issue of shares not being included in the EPS was an oversight by the directors, and also the treatment of issue costs is often quite complex and misunderstood. EPS is significantly reduced and is unlikely to be favoured by the directors.

The treatment of the bonus element in the post-balance rights issue is a difficult technical issue which again the directors might have not been aware of.

Overall, the original EPS of $0.80 calculated by the directors should now be reported as a loss per share of $0.082. It is unlikely that the directors have been guilty of fraud or deliberate window dressing, but they have clearly not followed several accounting standards, and the auditors have an obligation to qualify the accounts accordingly.

Solution 2.6: Shiplake

(a)   Definition of an impairment and when an impairment review should be carried out

An impairment loss arises where the carrying value of an asset, or group of assets, is higher than their recoverable amounts. In effect, the standard requires that assets should not appear on a balance sheet at a value which is higher than they are 'worth'. The recoverable amount of an asset is defined as the higher of its net realisable value (i.e. the amount at which it can be sold for net of direct selling expenses) and its value in use (i.e. its estimated future net cash flows discounted to a present value). IAS 36 *Impairment of Assets* recognises that many assets do not produce independent cash flows, and therefore the value in use may have to be calculated for a group of assets – a cash generating unit.

The standard recognises that it would be too onerous for companies to have to test for impaired assets every year, and therefore only requires impairment reviews when there is some indication that an impairment has occurred. The exception to this general principle is where goodwill or other intangible assets are being depreciated over a period of more than 20 years, in which case an impairment review is required at least annually. This also applies where any tangible non-current asset, other than land, has a remaining life of more than 50 years.

(b) The circumstances that indicate that a company's assets have been impaired

Impairments generally arise where there has been an event or change in circumstances. It may be that something has happened to the assets themselves (e.g. physical damage) or there has been a change in the economic environment relating to the assets (e.g. new regulations may have come into force). The standard gives several examples of indicators of impairment, which may be available from internal or external sources:

(i) Poor operating results. This could be a current operating loss or a low profit. One year's losses in itself does not necessarily mean there has been an impairment, but if this is coupled with previous losses or expected future losses then this is an indication of impairment.

(ii) A significant decline in an asset's market value (in excess of normal depreciation though use or the passage of time) or evidence of obsolescence (through market changes or technology) or physical damage.

(iii) Evidence of a reduction in the useful economic life or estimated residual value of assets.

(iv) Adverse changes in the market or economy, such as the entry of a major competitor, new statutory or regulatory rules or any indicator of value that has been used to value an asset (e.g. on acquisition a brand may have been valued on a 'multiple of sale revenues'. If subsequent sales were below expectations, this may indicate an impairment).

(v) A commitment to a significant reorganisation or restructuring of the business.

(vi) Loss of key employees or major customers

(vii) Increases in long-term interest rates (this could materially impact on value in use calculations thus affecting the recoverable amounts of assets).

(viii) Where the carrying amount of an enterprise's net assets are more than its market capitalisation.

(c) How the information would affect the preparation of Shiplake's consolidated financial statements

(i) *Goodwill*

On the acquisition of a subsidiary, the purchase consideration must be allocated to the fair value of its net assets with the residue being classed as goodwill (or negative goodwill if the assets have a greater fair value than the purchase consideration). IFRS 3 *Business Combinations* recognises that it is not always possible accurately to determine the value of some assets at the date of acquisition, and therefore allows an 'investigation period' up to the end of the first full reporting period following the period of acquisition. As the revision to the value of Halyard's assets was due to more detailed information becoming available, the fall in its asset values should be treated as an adjustment to the provisional valuations made at the time of acquisition. In effect, the net assets and goodwill should be restated to $7 million and $5 million respectively; the fall of $1 million is not an impairment loss and should not be charged to the income statement. This revision will have the effect of increasing the amortisation of goodwill from $800,000 to $1 million per annum (based on a 5-year life) (using pre IFRS 3 Amortisation Policy). The above assumes that the recoverable value of the company as a whole is greater than $12 million.

The fall in value of Mainstay's assets is the result of events that occurred after the acquisition (i.e. physical damage to the plant), and this does constitute an impairment loss. The plant and machinery should be written down to its recoverable amount, and the loss charged to the income statement. On the assumption that the recoverable value of the company as a whole has not fallen, goodwill will not be affected.

(ii) *Earth-moving plant*

On the basis of the original estimates, Shiplake's earth-moving plant was not impaired, the value in use of $500,000 being greater than its carrying value, However, due to the 'dramatic' increase in interest rates causing Shiplake's cost of capital to increase, the value in use of the plant will have to be recalculated. As the discount rate has risen, this will cause the value in use to fall. There is insufficient information to be able to quantify this fall. If the new discounted value is above the carrying value $400,000, there is still no impairment. If it is between $245,000 and $400,000, this will be the recoverable amount of the plant and it should be written down to this value. As the plant can be sold for $250,000 less selling costs of $5,000, $245,000 is the least amount that the plant should be written down to even if its revised value in use is below this figure.

(iii) *Research and development*

The treatment of the research and development costs in the year to 31 March 2001 was correct due to the element of uncertainty at the date. The development costs of $75,000 written off in that same period should not be capitalised at a later date even if the uncertainties leading to its original write-off are favourably resolved. The treatment of the development costs in the year to 31 March 2002 is incorrect. The directors' decision to continue the development is logical as (at the time of the decision) the future costs are estimated at only $10,000 and the future revenues are expected to be $150,000. It is also true that the project is now expected to lead to an overall deficit of $135,000 $(120 + 75 + 80 + 10 - 150$ (in $000)). However, at 31 March 2002 the unexpensed development costs of $80,000 are expected to be recovered. Provided the criteria in IAS 38 *Intangible Assets* are met, these costs of $80,000 should be recognised as an asset in the balance sheet and 'matched' to the future earnings of the new product. Thus the directors' logic of writing off the $80,000 development cost at 31 March 2002 because of an expected overall loss is flawed. The directors do not have the choice to write off the development expenditure.

(iv) Klassic Cars

An impairment loss relating to a cash generating unit should be allocated on the following basis:

1. To any obviously impaired assets (franchise costs)
2. To goodwill
3. To the remaining assets on a *pro rata* basis.

However, no asset should be written down to less than its net realisable value. Applying this to the impairment loss of $130 million ($370m − $240m):

	Cost $000	Impairment $000	Restated value $000
Goodwill	80,000	(80,000)	nil
Franchise costs	50,000	(20,000)	30,000 NRV
Restored vehicles	90,000	nil	90,000 NRV
Plant	100,000	2/3 (20,000)	80,000
Other net assets	50,000	1/3 (10,000)	40,000
	370,000	(130,000)	240,000

Note: the franchise cost cannot be written down to less than its realisable value, the restored vehicles have a realisable value higher than their cost and should not be written down at all, and the remaining impairment loss (after the goodwill and franchise write downs) of $30 million is apportioned *pro rata* to the plant and the other net assets.

Solution 2.7: Nettle

Report to the directors of Nettle on the potential impact of key events affecting the company

(i) IASC restructuring

The International Accounting Standards Committee approved a new constitution in March 2000. The new institution took immediate effect, and provides for the transition between the current and new structures. There are strong indications that the estimated budget of between $50 and $60 million is reasonable, and that stakeholders around the world are willing to contribute sufficient funds to permit IASC to function. Major international accounting firms, stock exchanges, international banks and financial institutions are supporting the IASC financially. The IASs have been endorsed by the Basel Committee, and subsequently by the International Organisation of Securities Commissions (IOSCO). The IOSCO endorsement will lead to improved global financial reporting, benefiting not only users but also preparers in global capital markets because it will cover global standard setting towards one international accounting language. The IASC has recently changed its official name to the International Accounting Standards Board (IASB), and it is now issuing International Financial Reporting Standards (IFRS).

The future standard-setting board of 14 independent, technical persons will have sole responsibility for the agenda of standard setting, and for setting the standards. The Board will not be dominated by any particular constituency or regional interest. Thus the reorganisation of the IASB comes at a time when the Board is at its strongest and at a time when International Standards are being accepted by more national and international entities. IASB is in a very strong position to take on its global responsibilities, and the reorganisation of the IASB has thus strengthened rather than weakened its position. Further, the European Commission has set out proposals which will require all European Union companies listed on a regulated market to prepare consolidated financial statements in accordance with International Standards by 2005. This shows the degree of confidence that major institutions have in IASB.

(ii)   Share options

The accounting treatment of share options is a very contentious area. The charging of income statements with the fair value of options issued caused significant political repercussions for US standard setters. In the UK, UITF17 *Employee Share Schemes* applied until FRS 20 was published, as a result any options granted at a discount to the market price required the discount to be charged to the income statement. Usually this amount is zero because the option is not written at a price less than the present market price, as in the case of Nettle's options ($7 per share). Of course, options written on such terms are not worthless. Their value is based upon the prospect of a rise in the share price. There are two accepted methods of recognising and measuring employee share option schemes: the 'intrinsic value method' and the 'fair value based method'. IAS 19 *Employee Benefits* does not specify recognition and measurement requirements for such benefits because of the lack of international consensus. However, IAS 19 does require the disclosure of equity compensation benefits in order that users can assess their effect on the financial statements.

However, the IASC (now IASB) has issued IFRS 2 *Share-Based Payment*, and this proposes to charge the income statement with the fair value of the options, measured at the 'grant date', which is the date at which the recipients are awarded rights to the options. The fair value will include the time value of the option, and there is therefore likely to be a significant amount charged in the income statement over the period during which employees earn their rights to take up the options.

Year ended 30 September 2001:

		Options vested or due to vest on	
		30 Sep 2001	**30 Sep 2002**
(i)	Number of options	2 million	3 million
(ii)	Fair value of option per share	$2	$3
(iii)	Relevant service completed	100%	50%
(iv)	Proportion vested or expected to vest	90%	96%
	Charge (i) $\times$ (ii) $\times$ (iii) $\times$ (iv)	$3.6 million (a)	$4.32 million (b)
	Total charge for year (a) + (b)	$7.92 million	

Thus, under IFRS 2, the income statement will be charged with $7.92 million in the current year. The accrual should be shown as part of equity. If the employees do not exercise their options and the options lapse, no adjustment is made to the transaction amount, as the IASB feel that at the date of grant the transaction is complete. The idea is that the options have been earned by the employees and have been issued by the company. Based on the above figures, an additional $4.32m will be charged in the income statement for the year ending 30 September 2002, when the relevant service period is completed. This figure will not change with any movement in the fair value of the option, but will be adjusted for any changes in the expected proportion of employees achieving their performance targets.

If the employees exercise the options, then the cash subscribed for the shares will be split between share capital and share premium account. Services of the employee do not normally form part of the consideration received for the shares issued, and thus the accrual will remain in reserves.

Options are much harder to value at the granting date, but it seems more sensible to use this date as this is the date where the transaction was perceived to have occurred by yourselves and the employees. It is worth remembering that the issue of share options will affect the diluted earnings per share calculation.

(iii)   Impairment of assets

The entrance of the major competitor in the marketplace and the occurrence of the change in profitability may indicate that impairment in the value of non-current assets and goodwill has occurred. These circumstances will trigger an impairment review under IAS 36 *Impairment of Assets*, which involves the comparison of the carrying value of the net assets with their value in use.

The following discussion is based upon the assumption that the merged operations are a single combined cash generating unit. When the competitor organisation was merged with the existing business, the result was that both purchased and unrecognised internally generated goodwill were contained in the merged business.

Leaf	Acquisition cost		150
	Fair value of net assets		(130)
	Goodwill		20
Nettle	Value in use at acquisition		250
	Fair value of assets at acquisition		(240)
Internally generated goodwill			10

As there are circumstances which have indicated the potential impairment of goodwill, then an impairment test must be carried out even though the first year review was satisfactory. The IASB in IAS 36 *Impairment of Assets* agrees with the theory behind the principle that any impairment loss should exclude internally generated goodwill (para. B104 IAS36). However, because of the cost and difficulty of distinguishing items relating to internally generated goodwill (especially if businesses are merged), the Board has rejected the idea that any impairment loss be allocated between purchased and internally generated goodwill.

	$
Carrying amount of tangible net assets (130+180)	310
Carrying amount of goodwill	
($20 million − amortisation 2 years $8 million)	12
Total net asset value	322
Value in use	307
Impairment	15

$$\text{Value in use} = \frac{\$19 \text{ million}}{1.12} + \frac{\$26 \text{ million}}{1.12^2} + \frac{\$26 \text{ million} \times 1.02 \times 1.02}{0.08 \times 1.12^2}$$

$$= \$307 \text{ million}$$

The impairment is allocated first to purchased goodwill and then to tangible net assets. Thus purchased goodwill will be written down by $12 million and tangible net assets by $3 million. There will be an increase in the charge to the income statement of $15 million for the impairment loss.

Solution 2.8: Com

To determine whether an impairment of an asset has incurred, it is necessary to compare the carrying amount of the asset with its recoverable amount. The recoverable amount is the higher of net selling price and value in use. It is not always easy to estimate value in use. In particular, it is not always practicable to identify cash flows arising from an individual fixed asset. If this is the case, value in use should be calculated as the level of cash generating units. A cash generating unit is defined as a group of assets that generates cash and is largely independent of the reporting entity's other cash generating units.

The cash generating unit comprises all the sites at which the product can be made. Each business is a cash generating unit by itself. However, any impairment of individual businesses is unlikely to be material. A material impairment is likely to occur only when a number of businesses are affected together by the same economic factors. It may therefore be acceptable to consider groupings of businesses affected by the same economic factors, rather than each individual business.

Memorandum

From: Management Accountant
Date: 23rd May 2001
Subject: Effect of two transactions on the consolidated financial statements

Transaction 1

1.1 The fact that Novel has made losses since it was acquired by the group suggests that it may have suffered an impairment in value. Therefore IAS 36 *Impairment of Assets* requires the group to carry out an impairment review at 31 January 2001. The impairment review is carried out at company level because the company is treated as a single cash generating unit.

1.2 At 31 January 2001 the carrying value of the subsidiary in the consolidated financial statements is $51.5 million (*W1*). As the recoverable amount (value in use) is only $40 million, Novel has suffered an impairment loss of $11.5 million. IAS 36 requires that the loss is recognised immediately in the income statement, and that it is allocated first to goodwill and then to the other assets on a *pro rata* basis. No asset can be written down below its net realisable value.

1.3 The adjustment required to record the impairment is as follows:

Dr Income statement	$11,500,000	
Cr Goodwill		$8,000,000
Cr Development expenditure (1.5/56.5 × 3.5 million)		$92,920
Cr Property, plant and equipment (55/56.5 × 3.5 million)		$3,407,080

1.4 The current assets are not written down because their net realisable value is greater than their carrying value. (Note also that the development expenditure is not written down below its net realisable value.)

1.5 The impairment loss is material, and therefore it is disclosed separately as required by IAS 8 *Accounting Policies, Changes in Accounting Estimates and Errors*.

Transaction 2

2.1 You have accounted for the $2 million write down correctly. Beta has communicated its decision to accept payment of $8 million to Gamma, and has received this amount in settlement. Therefore it has entered into an obligation from which it cannot reasonably withdraw.

2.2 It could be argued that the bad debt of $2 million is material in the context of the group profit before tax. This suggests that the write-off may have to be separately disclosed as required by IAS 8.

2.3 Further details of this transaction should be disclosed in the notes to the group financial statements, despite the fact that the parent company was not directly involved.

2.4 Gamma is controlled by one of the directors of Beta, a company within the group, and this director is also able to influence the policies of Beta. Therefore Beta and Gamma are related parties as defined by IAS 24 *Related Party Disclosures*.

2.5 IAS 24 requires disclosure of the following information:
- The names of the related parties
- A description of the nature of the relationship between the parties
- A description of the transaction
- The elements of the transaction necessary for an understanding of the financial statements (the amounts involved; the amount due from Gamma at 31 January 2001; and the amount written off in respect of the debt).

Working

W1   Carrying value of Novel at 31 January 2001

	$000	$000
Net assets		43,500
Goodwill:		
Cost of investment	60,000	
Net assets acquired	(50,000)	
	10,000	
Less: amortisation (2 years)	(2,000)	
		8,000
		51,500

3

Asset valuation: accounting for intangible assets, inventories and construction contracts – solutions

Solution 3.1: Satellite

(a) Discuss how the four issues are dealt with in the group accounts

(i) Leases

Operating lease

The requirement of the lease that the building be returned in good condition means that there is an obligation to a third party which has occurred because of a past event, which is the signing of the lease. The obligation cannot be avoided. However, IAS 37 *Provisions, Contingent Liabilities and Contingent Assets* states that future repairs and maintenance costs are not present obligations resulting from past events, as they relate to the future operation of the business and therefore should be capitalised as assets or written off as operating expenses when incurred. However, the lessee may have to incur periodic charges for maintenance or make good dilapidations or other damage during the rental period. The recognition of such liabilities is not precluded by the standard if the event giving rise to the obligation under the lease has occurred. Thus in the case of Satellite, due to the severe weather damage, a provision for $1.2m should be set up.

Could a more general provision be built up over the 6 years for dilapidation costs? It could be argued that the event giving rise to the obligation under the lease is the passage of time, and therefore $1m ought to be provided for. It is possible to take a more narrow view which would require specific dilapidation before an obligation exists. In conclusion, there should be a provision of $1.2m for the renovating due to the exceptional weather damage and a further provision of $800,000 (($6m − $1.2m)/6) for the obligation under the lease as it cannot be avoided. If the operating lease was terminated immediately, then some expenditure would be required on the interior of the building and the exterior would require complete renovation. Thus the total provision required is $2m.

It is possible that if the spirit of IAS 37 were adopted, the provision required could be based on actual dilapidation in the year. This would be difficult to estimate, and may not be more accurate than the arbitrary allocation made above.

Finance lease

The finance lease relates to the warehouse, which must be restored to its original state when the lease expires. The obligation to restore the building to its original state arose when the sports facility was created. It appears that the company cannot avoid the reinstatement costs, and therefore full provision of $2m should be made. The company should set up a corresponding asset as the sports facility represents access to future economic benefits that are to be enjoyed over more than one period. The amount will be added to the finance lease costs and additional depreciation of 10% of $2m will be charged as follows:

			$000	$000
Dr		Group retained profits	160	
		Minority interest	40	
	Cr	Depreciation		200

The balance sheet value of the leased building ($8m + $2m − $200,000) = $9.8m. However, the recoverable amount of the lease is $9.5m, and therefore the asset is impaired and requires writing down to this amount:

Dr		Group retained profits	240	
		Minority interest	60	
	Cr	Leased asset		300

Owned assets

Major periodic repairs to non-current assets are not provided for under IAS 37. These repairs are not present obligations of the company, as they relate to the future operations of the company. If there is declining service potential then the asset should be depreciated to reflect this and expenditure on repairs and maintenance should be capitalised to reflect the restoration of service potential. Also, the repairs in the case of Satellite could be avoided by selling the buildings. Thus no provision for the $6m is made.

(ii)   Database

IAS 38 *Intangible Assets* sets out the criteria that should be met in order to recognise an internally generated intangible asset. An entity is required to demonstrate the technical feasibility of the asset, the ability to complete and use or sell the asset, the probable future economic benefits, and the availability of adequate technical, financial and other resources before it can be recognised. The asset must also be capable of being reliably measured.

IAS 38 prohibits the recognition of internally generated brands, mastheads, publishing titles and customer lists etc. as intangible assets. It could be argued that the database falls into this category, but because it is generating future income it is felt that recognition can occur. It should be recognised as the value of its future revenue earnings capacity (i.e. $2m). To date $3m is being amortised over 5 years, the same rate as goodwill. The adjustment should therefore be:

			$	$
Dr		Group retained profits	800,000	
		Minority interest	200,000	
	Cr	Intangible asset		1,000,000

Being the write down of development costs to $2m

			$	$
Dr		Intangible assets	600,000	
	Cr	Group retained profit		480,000
		Minority interest		120,000

Being the reversal of amortisation to date

			$	$
Dr		Group retained profits	400,000	
		Minority interest	100,000	
	Cr	Intangible asset		500,000

Being the amortisation of $2m over 4 years

(iii) Hedging

Satellite must comply with the disclosure requirements of IAS 32 *Financial Instruments: Disclosure and Presentation* and disclose its accounting policy in respect of hedge accounting, which will be to translate its foreign currency assets and liabilities at the forward rate at the date of delivery. Under this method no exchange gain or loss is recognised, and this reflects the fact that the company has eliminated all currency risks by entering into the contract. The forward premium interest in the contract (i.e. difference between forward rate and spot rate at 1.12.1999) is not separately identified.

The inter-company profit in inventory must be eliminated, as two-thirds of the inventory remains unsold. The value of the inventory in Satellite's books is $1m ((2/3 × 2.1m unos)/ 1.4), of which the inter-company element is $200,000. The accounting entries will be:

Dr	Income statement	200,000	
Cr	Inventory		200,000

Additionally, the company must disclose certain information about the hedge accounting gains and losses. This information is required by IAS 32. By taking out a forward contract, the company has fixed the cost of inventory at $1.5m based on the forward contract rate (2.1m unos/1.4).

Satellite has paid nothing to enter into the forward contract, and therefore its book and fair value at the inception date is zero. At 31 March 2000, the settlement date, there is a loss on the hedging contract of (2.1m unos at 1.45 − 2.1m unos at 1.4), i.e. $51,724. Part of this loss relating to the inventory sold (one-third) is recognised in income ($17,241). The balance of $34,483 is carried forward in inventory. This should be reduced by the inter-company element, i.e. 20% on selling price, and only $27,586 is disclosed as a deferred loss carried forward in the balance sheet. Also, based on the assumption that the remaining inventory will be sold next year, this figure should be shown as a loss which is expected to be recognised in the income statement in the following year.

(iv) Contingent consideration

The time limit for fair value adjustments set out in IFRS 3 *Business Combinations* applies only to the net assets acquired. There is no time limit imposed on the calculation of contingent consideration. Therefore, an additional amount of goodwill of $8m is recognised and a liability of $8m shown. The increase in goodwill should be amortised over the remaining useful life of 4 years as a change in estimate.

		$	$
Dr	Goodwill	6m	
	Group reserves	2m	
Cr	Creditors		8m

(b) Revised Group Balance Sheet as at 30 November 2000

	$000
Non-current assets	
Intangible assets (5,180 − 1,000 + 600 − 500 + 6,000)	10,280
Non-current assets (38,120 + 2,000 − 200 − 300)	39,620
	49,900
Net current assets (27,900 − 200 − 8,000)	19,700
Total assets less current liabilities	69,600
Capital and reserves	
Called up share capital	16,100
Share premium account	5,000
Accumulated profits	
(27,400 − 2,000 − 160 − 240 − 800 + 480 − 400 − 200 − 2,000)	22,080
Minority interests (9,100 − 40 − 60 − 200 + 120 − 100)	8,820
Non-current liabilities: interest bearing liabilities	12,700
Provisions for liabilities and charges (900 + 2,000 + 2,000)	4,900
	69,600

Solution 3.2: H

(a) Why it might be justifiable to capitalise research costs

There are a number of arguments in favour of a capitalisation policy:

1. Research expenditure will probably generate future revenue in the long term and should be matched against its associated revenue.
2. It can be argued that for every 40 projects there are 5–6 successful, and thus the costs of the unsuccessful projects should be regarded as part of the costs of the successful projects. They are necessary expenses to arrive at successful outcomes.
3. Research may not be successful immediately but could lead to valuable projects in the future, as this could eliminate problems at an early stage and thus ultimately contribute to successful outcomes.

(b) Why IAS 38 imposes rigid rules for capitalisation of development expenditure

Development expenditure can be material and can considerably affect reported profit and net assets. If there were no rules it would be too subjective as to what costs could be capitalised, and this would lead to a lack of comparability across reporting entities. The key characteristics of good reporting insist that both relevance and reliability be taken into consideration when assessing the most appropriate policy to undertake.

(c) Are the requirements of IAS 38 likely to discourage investment in research and development?

The issue of capitalisation or not is unlikely to determine the economic decision as to whether or not development should be undertaken. IAS 38 requires expenditure to be capitalised if it meets certain criteria, unless in the USA where it is always expensed and in the UK where it may be capitalised or written off immediately. IAS 38 thus encourages capitalisation.

Even if certain research fails to meet the specified criteria for capitalisation, it is still possible for the management team to use the Director's Report and Operating and Finance Reviews to explain how much they have invested in individual projects during the year. The reasons for undertaking the projects can also be explained in narrative terms.

There is a problem if investors merely look at the bottom line without getting behind the figures, and if management believe that to be the case it may possibly discourage research.

(d) The advantages and disadvantages of offering a 'fair presentation override'

Reporting entities who are preparing financial statements under international financial reporting standards are required to comply with every applicable accounting standard. However, there are 'rare circumstances' when an entity must diverge from those standards if it feels it necessary to provide a fairer presentation of the financial statements. This is covered in IAS 1.

The benefits of adopting the fair presentation override should include more reliable and relevant information for the company's investors, otherwise the financial statements could lose credibility.

There are a number of major disadvantages in applying the override:

1. It is possible that some unscrupulous companies might use the override to justify an unacceptable accounting treatment, so it is important that auditors require the companies to disclose why the standards should not be applied and why an alternative could be adopted instead.
2. It could be argued that by having to adopt the override the ASB's original standards were themselves misleading, which could undermine their very existence. It must be remembered, however, that the override should only be applied on rare occasions.

Solution 3.3: S

(a) Effect of treating a lease as operating rather than finance

If the lease is treated as an operating lease rather than a finance lease, the main differences will be seen on the balance sheet. As a finance lease, the asset is shown as a non-current asset on the balance sheet together with a related liability. If the lease is an operating lease, then there is no capitalisation of an asset, nor a liability created.

In the income statement the difference between the two treatments is not so significant. If the lease is treated as an operating lease, then the full lease rental will appear as an expense in the income statement. However, if the lease is treated as a finance lease, the lease payment is split between the interest element and the capital repayment. Only the interest element is shown as the finance cost in the income statement. However, as the asset has been treated as a non-current asset under the finance lease, then the income statement will also have a charge for depreciation each year.

The two main ratios that may be affected by the treatment of the lease are return on capital employed, and gearing. Return on capital employed is calculated as net profit before interest divided by capital employed. The net profit is likely to be similar whether the lease is treated as an operating or a finance lease. If the net profit before interest is used, then the capital employed figure is the equity capital plus any long-term loan providers. Part of the finance lease will appear in non-current liabilities and therefore will be part of capital employed, reducing the return on capital employed.

(b)   Should the lease be accounted for as an operating or a finance lease?

IAS 17 *Leases* requires a lease to be treated as a finance lease if substantially all of the risks and rewards of ownership are transferred to the lessee. An important element of evidence of the transfer of risks and rewards is whether the lessee has the use of the asset for substantially all of its useful life. The terms of S's lease with C Bank is such that it is almost definite that S will have the use of the asset for all of its useful life. The asset is vital to the production process and the cost of refurbishing it is prohibitively expensive, therefore it is almost certain that S will continue for the entire 6 years of the lease. Therefore the lease should be treated as a finance lease.

(c)   How does the classification affect gearing ratios?

A company's financial statements are important sources of information for shareholders, potential shareholders and potential providers of loan capital. The balance sheet shows the financial position of the company at the year end, and is an important indicator to these users of the state of the company. The position shown by the balance sheet will affect the perceptions and decision making of the users of the financial statements.

If the balance sheet shows increased levels of gearing, then this could have the effect of causing a fall in the share price as shareholders perceive the company as introducing further risk. The increased perceived level of gearing may also mean that potential providers of loan capital will require higher rates of interest in order to combat the increased gearing and risk.

Some providers of loan capital will include covenants which require the gearing ratio to be kept within certain limits. The inclusion of a lease as a finance lease may take the gearing ratio above this level, thereby meaning that the company is technically in default of its loan agreement.

However, most sophisticated users of financial statements are capable of understanding the economic reality that is behind the position shown in the balance sheet. If the lease is of benefit to the company, then how it is portrayed in the balance sheet should theoretically have no effect on the perceptions of the users of the financial statements. Whether the lease were classified and recorded as an operating lease or a finance lease should have no effect on the company despite the gearing implications, as the underlying economic reality will be discovered by users from their study of the financial statements and the notes that accompany them.

(d)   Do the rules enable creative accounting to exist?

The preparation of financial statements is governed by a wide variety of International Accounting Standards covering both specific and general areas of accounting. If consideration is taken of both the specific and general accounting standards, there are very few areas of accounting that will not fall under the remit of an accounting standard. However, although now difficult, it is still possible to influence the profit figure or the balance sheet position in a number of ways.

One example is the possible treatment of the lease in S. By choosing to treat the lease as an operating lease, the directors of S were taking a very literal approach to IAS 17 by treating each 2-year period effectively as a separate lease. It is unlikely that S's auditors would agree to this treatment.

A possibly easier approach is to bias the figures whilst remaining within the spirit of an accounting standard. For example, IAS 16 *Property, Plant and Equipment* allows a company to choose the most appropriate method of depreciation for its fixed assets and the best estimate of useful economic life. By choosing a long useful economic life the annual depreciation charge can be reduced, or by choosing a high percentage reducing balance method of depreciation there can be large depreciation charges in the early years of the asset's life and much lower charges in later years.

Solution 3.4: Lease

(a)   Reasons why standard setters are proposing capitalisation of operating leases

Operating lease finance is used by a large number of companies. It is used for short-term financing of cars and long-term financing of land and buildings. Companies seek to preserve scarce capital and 'rent' resources rather than own them. They will not own the leased assets, but will incur significant obligations under lease arrangements. A major deficiency of current accounting standards is that they do not require recognition in the lessee's balance sheets of material assets and liabilities arising from operating leases.

Because operating leases do not appear on the balance sheet, companies have drawn up leasing agreements which are essentially finance leases as 'off balance sheet' operating leases. If balance sheets are to represent faithfully an entity's assets and liabilities, then operating leases ought to be shown on the balance sheet. Current standards have promoted the structuring of financial arrangements so as to meet the classification of an operating lease so that the effects of capitalisation are avoided in financial statement ratios. The ability to achieve this 'off balance sheet' treatment detracts from the comparability and usefulness of financial statements. The 'off balance sheet' effect is so material that it cannot be ignored if there is to be meaningful analysis of financial statements.

Current lease standards make it clear that quantitative criteria are to be used as guidance only, and that the determination of whether a lease is to be classified as a finance lease or operating lease is a matter of professional judgement. However, in practice, quantitative criteria have been perceived as precise rules and in some cases have been applied as absolute thresholds. Thus the intent of standards has been thwarted by leasing arrangements being packaged to fail, by a small margin, any specific quantitative tests for classification as a finance lease.

Opposing conclusions can be reached when trying to assess the substance of the agreement, such as the relative responsibilities of lessors and lessees for maintenance, insurance and the bearing of losses. This can lead to similar leases being classified differently. Thus the arbitrary and judgemental nature of standards and the ease with which such standards can be circumvented, have led to calls from standard setters to bring operating leases onto the balance sheet.

There is disclosure of future operating lease commitments so that it is possible to make an 'inspired' assessment of operating lease assets and liabilities. Thus the market can 'price in' the effect of capitalising operating leases, which leads one to ask why companies are afraid of showing such commitments on the balance sheet in the first place?

(b)   Effect on income statement and balance sheet

Income statement after adjustment for capitalisation of operating leases

		$m
		$m
Profit on ordinary activities before taxation	88	
Add back operating lease rentals	40	
Less depreciation (*W1*)	(28)	
Profit before taxation		100
Taxation on profit on ordinary activities		
(30 + 30% of 40 − 28)		(33.6)
		66.4

Balance sheet after adjustment for capitalisation of operating leases

	$m
Non-current assets (200 + 404 + 32 − 28 depr.) (*W1*)	608
Net current assets (170 − 35 operating lease liability − 3.6 extra tax)	131.4
	739.4
Share capital	200
Accumulated profits (120 + 66.4 revised income − 58 original income)	128.4
	328.4
Non-current liabilities (50 + 436 op. lease − 40 rental − current liab. 35)	411
	739.4

Working

W1 Net present value of operating lease commitments

	Land and buildings $m		Motor vehicles $m	Total $m
30 November 2001 (28 × 95%)	26.7	(9 × 95%)	8.6	35.3
30 November 2002 (25 × 95% × 95%)	22.6	(8 × 95% × 95%)	7.3	29.9
30 November 2003 (20 × 85.734%)	17.3	(7 × 85.73%)	6.0	23.3
Thereafter (500 × 61.4%)	307.0			307.0
	373.6		21.9	395.5
Rentals 30 November 2000	30		10	40
	403.6		31.9	435.5
Rounded	404		32	436
Depreciation (5%/25%)	20		8	28

Note: The $35m due at 30 November 2001 should be recorded as a current liability.

(c)   Impact on accounting ratios

The capitalisation of operating leases has a major impact on the critical performance measures. The net profit margin has increased from 15.2% to 17.2%, which is almost certainly a significant increase. This increase represents the increase in the profit arising from the replacement of the operating lease charges with depreciation on the capitalised leased assets.

The impact on Return on Capital Employed (ROCE) is quite dramatic. The ROCE falls from 23.8% to 13.5% due to the capitalisation of the operating leases. However, the most striking impact is on the gearing ratio, which increases from 16% to 125%.

The company would be concerned at the absolute changes in the ratios, but most performance assessments are based on comparisons with other 'similar' companies or industry averages. It is likely that the relative performance and financial risk within the sector is going to be substantially affected by the capitalisation of operating leases, as it is unlikely that all companies will use this form of finance to the same extent and over the same lease terms. American corporations monitor ROCE particularly closely and the dramatic decline may be of concern to the holding company, particularly if they are considering selling the company. Operating lease rentals are allowable for taxation and if capitalised these agreements attract tax allowances (depreciation and finance cost) which in this case are less than the rentals. The finance cost for the year is zero. This results in an increase in the tax payable for the period.

Lease may consider some other form of financing the usage of land and buildings, and motor vehicles. Sale and leaseback agreements will be affected by the capitalisation rules. However, motor vehicles can remain off the balance sheet by using 'Personal Contract Plans' whereby finance houses purchase the vehicles and sell the vehicles on to an employee. If operating leases are to be capitalised, the finance industry will probably create an instrument, which will still enable certain assets to remain off the balance sheet.

Whether the capitalisation of operating leases will affect the company's value or share price is debatable. There is already disclosure of future operating lease rentals so that analysts can already estimate the net present value of the liability, so it can be argued that this information is already priced in the market. The problem arises with those users of financial statements who are not so well informed of the complexities of financial statements.

Working – ratios

	Before capitalisation	**After capitalisation**
Net profit margin		
$\dfrac{\text{Profit before tax}}{\text{Turnover}}$	$(88/580) \times 100 = 15.25\%$	$(100/580) \times 100 = 17.2\%$
Return on capital employed		
$\dfrac{\text{Profit before tax}}{\text{Share capital} + \text{Reserves} + \text{Lt liabs}}$	$(88/370) \times 100 = 23.8\%$	$(88/739.4) \times 100 = 13.5\%$
Gearing		
$\dfrac{\text{Long-term liabilities}}{\text{Share capital} + \text{Reserves}}$	$(50/320) \times 100 = 16\%$	$(411/328.4) \times 100 = 125\%$

Solution 3.5: Petroplant

(a) Income statement and balance sheet

Income statement

	30 September 2000	30 September 2001	30 September 2002	Total
	$m	**$m**	**$m**	**$m**
Contract revenue	(*W1*) 375	(*W2*) 663	(*W3*) 677	(*W3*) 1,715
Cost of sales	(300)	(510)	(570)	(1,380)
Profit	75	153	107	335

Balance sheet

	30.09.2000	30.09.2001	30.09.2002
	$m	**$m**	**$m**
Current assets – amounts due from customers (*W4*)	95	nil	nil
Current liabilities – amounts due to customers (*W4*)	nil	62	nil

Working

W1 *Year ended 30 September 2000*
 Estimated total profit on the contract: $1,500 agreed price − 1,200 costs = $300m
 Costs to date: $300/$1200 = 25%
 Revenue to date: $1,500 × 25% = $375m

W2   *Year ended 30 September 2001*

Estimated total revenue on contract:

$1,500 × 102% = $1,530 + $200m variation	1,730m
Estimated total costs: $1,230 + $120m variation	1,350m
Estimated total profit:	$380m
Costs to date ($740 + $70)	$810m
Percentage complete ($810m/1,350m)	60%
Cost of sales ($810 − $300 2001)	510m
Contract revenue ($1,730 × 60% = $1,038m − $375m 2001)	663m

W3   *Year ended 30 September 2002*

Total revenue on contract $1,500 × 3% labour = $1,545 less 2% penalty 30	$1,515m
Variation	200m
	1,715m
Actual costs (1,265 + 115)	(1,380m)
Actual total profit	335m

W4   *Balance sheets*

	30.9.2000			30.9.2001			30.9.2002
	$m			**$m**			**$m**
Contracts costs to date	300	(300 + 510)		810	(810 + 570)		1,380
Profit recognised	75	(75 + 153)		228	(228 + 107)		335
	375			1,038			1,715
Progress billings paid	(280)			(1,100)			(1,715)
Amounts due from customers	95			–			–
Amounts due to customers	–			62			–

(b)   Contract variation

IAS 11 *Construction Contracts* argues that a variation of a contract should be treated as a separate contract where the asset differs in design, technology or function from the original asset. IAS 11 also argues that a variation in a contract is an instruction by the customer for a change in the scope of the work to be performed. In this case, the variation is a genuine variation of the original contract.

Solution 3.6: S

(a)   Calculation of figures in S's income statements and balance sheets

Income statement extracts

	$000
Turnover (750 + 2,250)	3,000
Cost of sales (580 + 1,900)	2,480
Provision for expected losses	(650)

Balance sheet extracts

Amounts recoverable under contracts	150
Provision for expected losses	(650)

Deep sea fishing boat

		2001			2002
		$000			**$000**
Total contract price		3,000			3,000
Total estimated costs (650 + 1,300)		1,950	(650 + 580 + 790)		2,020
Total estimated profit		1,050			980

Income statement

Proportion of work completed to 30.9.2001	900	(30% × 3,000)	(55% × 3000)	1,650	750
Costs incurred to 30.9.2001	650		(650 + 580)	1,230	580
Estimated profit to date	250			420	170

Balance sheets

	30.9.2001	30.9.2002	
	$000	**$000**	
Contracts costs to date	650	1,230	(650 + 480)
Profit recognised	250	420	(250 + 170)
	900	1,650	
Progress billings paid	800	1,500	(800 + 700)
Amounts due from customers	100	150	
Amounts invoiced not received	100	50	

Small passenger ferry

		2001		2002
		$000		**$000**
Total contract price		nil		5,000
Total estimated costs (nil + nil)		nil	(1,900 + 3,400)	5,300
Total estimated loss		nil		(300)

Income statement

	2001		2002
Proportion of work completed to 30.9.2001	nil	(45% × 5,000)	2,250
Costs incurred to 30.9.2001	nil	(nil + 1,900)	1,900
Estimated profit to date	nil		350

Balance sheets

	30.9.2001	30.9.2002
	$000	**$000**
Contracts costs to date	nil	1,900
Profit recognised	nil	350
	nil	2,250
Progress billings paid	nil	2,250
Amounts due from customers	nil	nil
Amounts invoiced not received	nil	nil
Provision for estimated losses		650

(b)   Recognising losses

The IASC's Framework defines liabilities as present obligations the settlement of which is expected to result in an outflow from the enterprise of resources embodying economic benefits. Under IAS 11 *Construction Contracts*, where there is an expected loss on a construction contract it must be provided for in full immediately the entity becomes aware of it. It is essentially an onerous contract from which the entity cannot withdraw and must settle. It is essentially a legal obligation, and therefore the definition of losses contained in the Framework can be used to justify the requirement of IAS 11 to recognise losses as soon as they are foreseen.

4

Balance sheet: liabilities – solutions

Solution 4.1: Genpower

(a) Why is there a need for an accounting standard on provisions?

The use of provisions can have a significant impact on a company's financial statements. They arise in many areas of business, and often relate to controversial aspects such as restructuring costs, environmental and decommissioning liabilities. They have often been set up based on management intentions rather than on the existence of a genuine liability.

In the recent past there has been much criticism of the use and abuse of provisions. The main abuse has been that of 'profit smoothing'. In essence this amounts to creating a provision, usually for some intended expenditure, when a company's profits are healthy, and subsequently releasing the provision through the income statement to offset the expenditure when it occurs. This has the effect of reducing the profit in the years in which provisions are made and increasing profits in years they are released. It is known as 'big bath accounting'. It means that provisions created for a specific purpose are aggregated with other provisions and subsequently used to offset expenditures of future years that were not (and should not have been) provided for. Such provisions were often very large and treated as extraordinary or exceptional items. This treatment may have caused some users to disregard the expense in the belief that it was a non-recurring item, thus minimising the adverse impact of the provision. Extreme cases occurred where provisions were deliberately over provided with the intention that their release in future years would boost profits.

In some cases provisioning was used to 'create' profits rather than just smooth them. This occurs if a provision is created without it being charged to the income statement before its subsequent release. The most common examples of this were provisions for restructuring costs as a consequence of an acquisition. The effect of such provisions was that they added to the goodwill rather than being charged to income. This practice created the ironic situation that (given an agreed purchase price) the more restructuring a company needed and the larger its anticipated losses were, the greater was the reported value of the acquired company's goodwill.

(b) Recognition criteria for provisions

IAS 37 is intended to establish appropriate recognition and measurement criteria for provisions and contingent assets and liabilities, as well as more extensive disclosure. Although not specifically referred to in the IAS, it does not apply to write downs of assets (e.g. bad debt provisions) or those provisions covered by more specific standards (e.g. deferred tax, pensions).

A provision is defined as a liability of uncertain timing or amount. It is also either a legal or constructive obligation which will probably require a transfer of economic benefits as a result of a past transaction or event.

A contingent liability is a possible obligation which will be confirmed only by the occurrence or non-occurrence of uncertain future events that are not wholly within the entity's control, or where an obligation cannot be reliably measured. A contingent asset is a 'mirror' of that of a 'contingent liability'.

An event is an obligating one if there is no realistic possibility of it being avoided. This is obviously the case if it is enforceable by law, but IAS 37 adds to this by introducing the concept of a constructive obligation. A constructive obligation derives from an established pattern of past practice or some form of public commitment to accept certain responsibilities that creates a valid expectation on the part of other parties that the entity will discharge them. Although the concept of a constructive obligation does introduce an element of subjectivity, the new definition is intended to prevent provisions being made as a result of future management intentions.

Reliable measurement is taken to be the best estimate of the expenditure required to settle the obligation at the balance sheet date. The estimate may be based on a range of possible outcomes, and it should take into account any surrounding risk and uncertainty, and the time value of money, if material. Where there are similar obligations (e.g. warranties), the estimate should be based on the class as a whole. The IAS considers that the circumstances in which a reliable estimate cannot be made will be rare, but if they exist, the liability should be treated as contingent and appropriately disclosed in the notes.

(c)   Environmental costs

Genpower's current policy of providing for environmental costs *re* demolition of the power station and 'sealing of fuel rods' is not acceptable under IAS 37. The standard requires that where a present obligation exists which will probably require a transfer of economic benefits, a provision should be made based on the best estimate of the full amount of the liability. If the liability is measured in expected future prices, it should be discounted at a nominal rate. The company should therefore provide $120m (not $180m) for environmental costs on 1 October 1999, as this is the date the obligation arose. An interesting aspect of the provision is the accounting entries. The credit entry is shown in the balance sheet as 'non-current liabilities', but the debit is included as part of the cost of the asset – i.e. power station. In effect, it grosses up the balance sheet by the amount of the liability and creates an asset of equivalent value.

The effect on the income statement is not too different from the original treatment, as the carrying value of the power station (inclusive of the provision) will be depreciated over its 10-year life and thus the former provision is effectively charged to income as additional depreciation.

The treatment of the provision for contamination leaks needs more careful consideration. It could be argued that the obligating event is the occurrence of a leak. As this has not happened, there is no liability and therefore a provision should not be made. An alternative view is that it is the generation of electricity that creates the possibility of a leakage and, as this has occurred, a liability should be recognised. The difference between a liability and a contingent liability is one of probability. If it is probable (i.e. more than 50% chance) then it is a liability that should be provided for. Conversely, if not probable it is a contingent liability which should be disclosed in the notes. In any 12-month period there is only a 30% chance of a contamination occurring. It could be argued that the liability is therefore not probable. Alternatively, it could be argued that statistically there will be three leakages causing contamination that will cost $90m. As the company has produced a tenth of the electricity, it should provide for a tenth of the expected contamination costs. On balance, and applying prudence, it would be acceptable to provide $9m for contamination costs each year.

Applying the above would give the following revised extracts:

	$m
Income statement charge	
Non-current asset depreciation 10% × ($200m + $120m)	32
Provision for contamination costs 10% × $90m or (30% × $90m)	9
	41
Balance sheet	
Property, plant and equipment	
Power station at cost ($200m + $120m)	320
Depreciation	(32)
	288
Non-current liabilities	
Provision for environment costs ($120m + $9m)	129

(d)   No environmental legislation

A constructive obligation occurs when there is a valid expectation by other parties that an entity will discharge its responsibilities. A constructive obligation usually derives from a company's actions. These may be in the form of an established pattern of past practice, a published policy statement, or by indications to other parties that it will accept certain responsibilities. If it can be established that Genpower has a publicly known policy of environmental cleaning up, or has a past record of doing so when it is not legally required to, then this could be taken as giving rise to a constructive obligation and the treatment of the environment costs would be the same as in part (c). If there is no legal requirement to incur the various environmental costs and Genpower has not created an expectation that it will be responsible for such costs, then there is no obligation and no provision should be made. The power station would be recorded at cost of $200m and depreciated at $20m per annum.

Solution 4.2: L

(a)   Identification of appropriate accounting treatment in order to comply with IAS 37

Packaging error

Under IAS 37, three conditions must be passed before a provision can be created on the packaging error:

1. There must be a legal or constructive obligation – clearly the company's lawyers believe this to be the case

2. There must be a probability that the claims will have to be paid – again this appears to be the case
3. The liability must be reliably measured – this has proved impossible to determine accurately and thus this condition has failed; it must therefore be treated as a contingent liability in the notes until such time as more information arises to determine the amount of the obligation.

Lotto claim for $200,000

Under IAS 37 all three conditions listed above appear to be met, and as the evidence has been received before the accounts have been authorised, under IAS 10 *Events After The Balance Sheet Date* the financial statements should be amended to take into account the new information. A provision for $200,000 should therefore be provided in the financial statements.

Winner card

Under IAS 37 it would appear that no legal or constructive obligation has arisen, since the police believe the claim to be a forgery and thus no payout will occur. It could be described as a remote contingent liability, but under IAS 37 these are totally ignored when preparing the financial statements.

Happy cards

Although it would appear that the company has no legal obligation to make good the losses suffered by the customers of their retailer in Newtown, they have decided as a goodwill measure to pay some compensation. However, the benefactors of this good news are not yet aware of that decision and thus have taken no action on it. It is therefore not strong enough to be classified as a contingent liability – it is a mere intention which the Directors could renege on in the future. It would not be permissible to include it in this year's financial statements as a liability. Not even a contingent liability disclosure is created.

(b) Paying attention to contingent liabilities

(i) Why is insufficient attention paid to contingent liabilities?

Most investors are not financially numerate, and they tend to look to the main primary statements for indicators of good or bad performance. In particular, the income statement is the key document. Rarely do investors go behind the figures and investigate the back-up notes. Usually the contingent liability note is found at the very back of the financial statements, so it would tend to be hidden from all bar the most perceptive of investors.

A more serious problem is the switch from full to the adoption of summarised financial statements which investors receive. They tend to concentrate on the main primary statements and may not include these very important contingent liabilities, which have the ability to be converted into substantial large 'real' liabilities in many cases.

The note published by companies does tend also to be very bland and may not even give an indication of the likely amount that could be paid if the situation were to go against the company. Often the note is deliberately vague to avoid giving away very sensitive information to prosecuting lawyers which could be used in court against the company.

(ii) *How does IAS 37 prevent companies from treating liabilities that should be on balance sheet from being merely noted as contingent?*

IAS 37 is a very strongly worded liability standard which applies in practice the foundations laid down in the Framework for recognising liabilities. That was done to prevent companies using provisions as 'big bath provisions' and deliberately trying to smooth out earnings by creating totally artificial liabilities on the balance sheet in good years which would subsequently be released back into profit in bad years.

IAS 37 achieves its objectives by insisting that liabilities may only be created when the reporting entity has a clear legal or constructive obligation to pay another party or to transfer over economic benefits to that party. A mere intention to transfer or pay is not permitted. The standard is therefore anti-prudence and will not permit artificial liabilities to be created.

It may be the situation, however, that the amount payable or the timing of the payment is uncertain. That does not prevent a provision being created, as reporting entities can usually work out from past experience or from expert legal or actuarial advice both the amount and timing of those likely transfers. Although these are clearly estimates, these can be investigated on an annual basis and with more evidence greater clarity will eventually emerge of the final amounts payable. These changes are recognised in the income statement as changes in accounting estimates.

However, if there is doubt over reliable estimation of the liability or only a possibility (say 50 : 50 chance) that a liability will be paid, then it should only be disclosed in the notes to the financial statement and not actually accrued on the balance sheet. If the chances of a loss are remote, then they should be ignored altogether.

Solution 4.3: Clean

(a) Explanation of why provision recognised by the directors

IAS 37 *Provisions, Contingent Liabilities and Contingent Assets* states that a provision should be recognised if all of the following conditions are met:

- there is a present obligation to transfer economic benefits as a result of a past transaction or event;
- it is probable that a transfer of economic benefits will be required to settle the obligation;
- a reliable estimate can be made of the amount of the obligation.

In Clean's position, two of the three conditions are clearly met. Clean will incur expenditure (i.e. transfer of economic benefits is virtually certain), and the directors have prepared detailed estimates of the amount.

Although Clean is not legally obliged to carry out the project, it appears that it has a constructive obligation to do so. IAS 37 states that an entity has a constructive obligation if both of the following apply:

- it has indicated to other parties that it will accept certain responsibilities by an established pattern of past practice or published policies;
- as a result, it has created a valid expectation on the part of those other parties that it will discharge those responsibilities.

Clean has a reputation of fulfilling its financial commitments once they have been publicly announced. Therefore the obligating event is the announcement of the proposal on 25 June 2000, the obligation exists at 30 June 2000 (the balance sheet date), and Clean is required to recognise a provision.

(b) Compute the appropriate provision in the balance sheets in respect of the proposed expenditure at 30 June 2000 and 30 June 2001

Provision as at 30 June 2000

		$m
Expenditure on:		
30 June 2001	$30m × 0.926 (8%)	27.78
30 June 2002	$30m × 0.857 (8%)	25.71
30 June 2003	$40m × 0.794 (8%)	31.76
		85.25

Provision as at 30 June 2001

		$m
Expenditure on:		
30 June 2002	$30m × 0.926	27.78
30 June 2003	$40m × 0.857	34.28
		62.06

(c) Compute the two components of the charge to the income statement for the year ended 30 June 2001

The charge to the income statement for the year ended 30 June 2001 consists of:

(i)   Depreciation ($85.25m/20 years) $4.2625m

This is reported within cost of sales.

The provision of $85.25m also represents an asset as it gives rise to future economic benefits (it enhances the performance of the factories). This is capitalised and depreciated over 20 years (the average useful life of the factories).

(ii)   Unwinding of the discount $6.81m

This is reported as a finance cost.

Working

	$m
Provision as at 1 July 2000	85.25
Expenditure on 30 June 2001	(30.00)
Unwinding of discount (bal. fig.)	6.81
Provision as at 30 June 2001	62.06

Or alternatively calculated:
$(30,000 - 27,780) = 2,220 + (27,780 - 25,710) + (34,280 - 31,760) = 6,810.$

(d) Evaluation of the extent to which financial statements prepared in accordance with IASs give useful information about the environmental policies of the reporting entity

International Accounting Standards (IASs) do not contain any specific requirements to disclose any information about an entity's environmental policies.

Because disclosure is voluntary, entities can disclose as much or as little information as they choose. There is nothing to prevent an entity from making disclosures in such a general way that they are meaningless, or from presenting information selectively. Disclosure is normally made in the Operating and Financial Review or in the Director's Report, and does not need to be audited.

Entities are required to disclose information about provisions and contingent liabilities relating to environmental matters, such as the cost of rectifying damage, decommissioning costs, and any claims for damages. They are also required to disclose information about large and unusual items recognised in the income statement. Therefore, any significant expenditure and the reason for it should be apparent. It may be possible to deduce some information about environmental policies from these disclosures.

In practice, an increasing number of large corporations choose to make extensive and extremely informative reports detailing their environmental policies and their performance in implementing them. This information is often audited. However, these disclosures normally take the form of a completely separate 'environment report', and are not included in the published financial statements themselves.

Solution 4.4: Z

(a) Explanation of why IAS 37 classifies contingencies between remote, possible, probable and virtually certain

IAS 37 effectively marries the two separate topics of contingencies and provisions into the one accounting standard. The common thread between the two is the word 'uncertainty'. There is uncertainty about the exact amount owing, when it will be paid, and also often the parties to which the amounts may have to be paid.

Effectively, contingent liabilities are defined as those that have less than a 50% chance of occurring or those whose value cannot be reliably measured. These are classified in the standard as either remote or possible. They are not strong enough to be recorded on the balance sheet. The remote contingencies are effectively ignored as they are unlikely ever to occur, but it is important for readers and investors of financial statements that possible liabilities be disclosed, as they could eventually have a major detrimental impact on the decision whether or not to invest in the company, and affect investors' perception of future performance or even viability.

IAS 37 forces companies that have probable contingent liabilities to classify these as provisions and they are therefore reported as liabilities on the balance sheet provided they can be reliably measured.

The term 'virtually certain' normally refers to contingent assets. These may only be recorded as real assets on the balance sheet if that term applies. A possible or probable contingent asset should never be recorded on the balance sheet, although the latter should be disclosed separately in the notes from any related contingent liability (known as reimbursements). The doctrine of prudence is still applied to the assets side of the balance sheet.

(b) Explanation as to how individual transactions should be accounted

Before investigating each of the transactions it should be noted that for a provision to be recorded on balance sheet the following conditions must be met:

- there must a clear legal or constructive obligation;
- there must be a probability of future economic benefits being transferred to another party; and
- the provisions must be reliably measured.

(i) Roof leak

There appears to be a legal obligation on the company, as the construction work was not satisfactory. It will probably have to be paid, and the amount of $100,000 can be reliably measured; thus a provision should be created for that amount with a related charge to profit and loss.

(ii) Roof installed by subcontractor

Any possible reimbursement from another party must be treated separately from the claim from the customer. The provision in (i) must still stand. Normally a probable recovery from a subcontractor would be treated either as an asset (if virtually certain) or in the notes as probable. However, the Chief Accountant has indicated that the subcontractor is almost insolvent and couldn't afford to pay for their faulty workmanship, and thus any reimbursement is extremely unlikely. In that case, no mention at all should even be made in the notes as to any likely contingent gain that might arise, despite the fact that the company appears to have a strong case for recovery.

(iii) Construction defects

These are normally rectification that occur in the contracting business. The company has a clear legal obligation to make good any defects. Normally each contract should be assessed at the end of the year and provision made for the likely amount still to be paid.

Because of past experience in the business, a reliable estimate of the amount due should be obtainable. They are similar to warranty provisions. The best evidence of the amount due at the year end is $120,000, and thus a further $40,000 needs to be provided on the balance sheet and an equivalent charge made against the income statement.

(iv) Delay in completion of electrical contract

The company has taken out a contract against a firm of electrical engineers for the delay they have caused in the completion of a contract. This can be recorded as an asset on the balance sheet if the amount is virtually certain and can be reliably measured. Although the Directors of the engineering company have agreed in principle to pay $30,000 compensation there is nothing in writing, and thus there is still some doubt on its recovery. It is a probable contingent asset, and therefore should be noted in the financial statements but not recorded on the balance sheet. If more evidence can be found to make it clear that the amount receivable is virtually certain, then it could be recorded as both an income of the period and as a full asset on the balance sheet. Prudence should normally dictate the recording of assets, so the current advice is to disclose only the amount due in the notes.

(v) Loss of laptop computer

There does not appear to be any liability at all for the lost files, as it would the responsibility of the architect to copy his or her files as well as keeping them on the laptop itself. The claim for $90,000 is therefore totally spurious and should be ignored, as the likelihood of it being paid is extremely remote. However, there is more of a legal obligation for the loss of the hardware, but the lawyers advising the company are of the opinion that the courts would only award nominal damages and it certainly would not be material in the overall context of the company's financial statements. It could therefore be argued to be remote and not even required to be mentioned in the notes.

Solution 4.5: Stonemaster

(a) Description of circumstances where a provision should be made

IAS 37 defines a provision as a liability of uncertain timing or amount. Provisions may only be recognised when:

1. There is a present obligation as a result of a past event. The obligation may be legal (i.e. enforceable by law) or it may be constructive. The latter arises when an entity has indicated that it will accept certain responsibilities even though it does not have a legal obligation to do so. This may be by a pattern of past practice or by some form of published statement.
2. It is probable that an outflow of resources will be required to settle the obligation.
3. The amount of the obligation can be reliably measured.

It should be extremely rare not to pass the latter condition. Also, a provision cannot be made unless all of the conditions are present. IAS 37 was intended to stamp out many of the abuses that existed in financial reporting in the past. These included the following.

Profit smoothing or big bath accounting

This is a technique whereby companies attempt to even out the trend of profits over several accounting periods to 'create' a trend of modest rising profits when the true trend may be much more volatile. This is achieved relatively simply by a company making a provision in one accounting period when profits are high and then releasing the provision in later years when profits are poorer. The provision was often made for a particular expenditure but then released to offset different expenditures.

IAS 37 prevents this in two ways – first, a provision can only be made if an actual liability exists, and secondly, a provision for one expenditure can no longer be used to offset different expenditures.

Creating profits

In some ways this is similar to big bath accounting except that the original provision was not charged to income. This occurred generally during acquisitions. An acquirer might create a large provision for reorganisation costs. This was treated as a liability of the acquired company, thus reducing the fair value of its net assets and increasing goodwill. The overall effect would be that the original provision bypassed the income statement (and added to goodwill) and post-acquisition profits were increased by the release of the provision. Ultimately the amortisation of goodwill would be charged against income, but over a very long period. IAS 37 specifically prohibits reorganisation provisions except where the acquiree's previous management had already announced a formal plan of restructuring.

(b) Stonemaster licence

There are two groups of liability in this example requiring different treatments. The decommissioning of the plant and removal of the temporary site buildings are liabilities that must be recognised immediately the assets are put on site, as this is the obligating event. The obligation must be created before any quarrying commences. The liabilities must be measured at present value, providing the best estimate of expenditures expected to settle the obligation. The 'unwinding' of the discount is treated as a finance cost. The value created is not charged initially to income but is instead added to the cost of the assets (i.e. plant and quarry). This has the effect of immediately recognising an obligation when it occurs, but charging it to income over the periods expected to benefit. The second group of liability is for the landscaping and roadway damage. These are costs that occur and increase via the extraction of stone from the quarry. These should be charged to income annually in proportion to the amount of stone extracted and damage caused.

The condition of the licence makes the above liabilities legally binding, and thus they cannot be avoided. If the licence had been granted without conditions, there would be no legal obligation. However, this does not necessarily mean that there is no obligation. It may be that Stonemaster has created a constructive obligation, perhaps by its past practice with similar environmental costs or by a published policy made in its financial statements or other public announcement. If this has created a valid expectation that Stonemaster will incur these costs, then the position is the same as above. If there is no constructive obligation, there would be no liability and no provisions could be made.

5

Performance measurement – solutions

Solution 5.1: Bosun

(a) Financial statements for Bosun

Income statement for Bosun for the year ended 31 March 2000

	$000
Sales revenue (2,800 − 120 − 600) (*W1* and *W2*)	2,080
Cost of sales (1,750 + 15 − 350) (*W1* and *W2*)	(1,415)
Gross profit	665
Operating costs (344 − 90 + 180) (*W2* and *W3*)	(434)
	231
Other operating income – finance lease interest (*W1*)	50
Finance costs (64 − 10 + 6)	(60)
	221
Income tax (150 − 60 − 54)	(36)
Profit after tax	185
Minority interests	(20)
	165
Dividends	(100)
Retained profit for the year	65

Balance sheet of Bosun as at 31 March 2000

	$000	$000
Non-current assets		
Property, plant and equipment	2,540	
Investment in finance leases (900 − 70) (*W1*)	830	
		3,370
Current assets		1,000
		4,370
Equity and liabilities		
Share capital and reserves:		
Equity shares of $1 each		1,200

Reserves:

Share premium (*W2*)	600	
Accumulated profits (1,134 − 500 *W2* + 65)	699	1,299
		2,499
Minority interest		140
Non-current liabilities		
12% Redeemable loan note (2004) (200 − 10 + 6 (*W4*))		196
Current liabilities (1,520 + 15 (*W1*))		1,535
Total equity and liabilities		4,370

Working

W1 Retail car sales

These must be accounted for under their substance. The finance cost is effectively included in the selling price, and should be removed as follows and accounted for under IAS 17 *Leases*:

	$'000 Dr	$'000 Cr
Sales revenue (100 × $1,200)	120	
Interest receivable		50
Investment in finance lease		70 (45 + 25)

Based on past experience of the cost of warranty claims, they should be provided at an amount of $15,000 (100 × $150) at the time of sale. This is also required under IAS 37 *Provisions, Contingent Liabilities and Contingent Assets*.

W2 Business combination under IFRS 3

Clearly the combination does not meet the 'pooling of interests' definition. This is now banned under IFRS 3, and thus acquisition accounting should be applied. The effect on Bosun's income statement would be to deduct $600,000 from sales, $350,000 from cost of sales, $90,000 from operating costs and $60,000 from income tax. This effectively removes $100,000 from net profit.

The purchase consideration was 200,000 shares × $4	$800,000
Net assets at date of acquisition	800,000
Goodwill	nil

A share premium of 200,000 × $3 = $600,000 is created, but retained profit is also reduced by the same amount ($500,000 prior years and $100,000 current year).

W3 Extraordinary item

Although a one-off item, compliance costs for the year 2000 are common to all companies and thus cannot be regarded as extraordinary. They could be classified as exceptional and be disclosed as an ordinary item in the notes. The $180,000 is added to operating costs.

W4 12% Redeemable loan notes

Initially these should be recorded at the net proceeds of issue, i.e. $190,000 ($200,000 less 5% discount.) The discount of $10,000 plus the final redemption premium of $20,000 should be regarded as finance costs to be charged through the income statement over the life of 5 years of the loan note. Thus $6,000 additional finance charge is required under IAS 32 *Financial Instruments: Presentation and Disclosure.*

(b) Calculation of Earnings Per Share

Basic EPS

Earnings: Earnings – profit after tax and minority interests = $165,000

Share structure: the number of shares existing for the full year, exclusive of those issued on last day, is 1 m, as 0.2 m was issued as part of the business combination

Basic EPS: ($165,000/1m shares) × 100 = 16.5c

Diluted EPS

Earnings:		
as per basic		$165,000
Share structure:		
as per basic	1m	
Options: 400,000 × $2/$4	0.2m	
		1.2m

Diluted EPS: ($165,000/1.2m shares) × 100 = 13.8c

Solution 5.2: Deltoid

(a) Balance sheet of Deltoid as at 31 March 2002

	$000	$000
Non-current assets		
Property, plant and equipment (12,110 + 600 − 20 (*W1*) − 120 (*W3*)		12,570
Current assets		
Inventory	3,850	
Trade accounts receivable	2,450	
Bank	250	6,550
Total assets		19,120
Equity and liabilities		
Share capital and reserves:		
Equity shares of $0.50 each (2,000 + 500 bonus issue)		2,500
Conversion rights (equity element loan note) (*W4*)		186
		2,686

Reserves:

Share premium	1,000	
Revaluation reserve (3,000 − 500 bonus issue)	2,500	
Accumulated profits (*W1*)	3,409	6,909
		9,595

Non-current liabilities

Environmental provision (1,200 + 950)	2,150
Finance lease (*W3*)	371
6% Convertible loan note (2,814 + 101 accrued interest)	2,915

Current liabilities

Trade accounts payable	2,820	
Accrued interest (*W3*)	24	
Finance lease (*W3*)	105	
Taxation	1,140	4,089
Total equity and liabilities		19,120

Note: The Directors have proposed a final dividend of $400,000 (*W5*).

Working

W1 Accumulated profits

	$000
Retained profit for the year (as per question)	2,000
Additional depreciation of plant (*W2*)	(20)
Additional depreciation of leased plant (*W3*)	(120)
Add rentals (*W3*)	150
Finance costs on loan notes (281 − 180 (*W4*))	(101)
Finance costs on leased plant (*W3*)	(50)
Additional environmental provision (245 − 180)	(65)
Restated retained profit for the year	1,794
Retained profit at 1.4.2001	2,500
Prior year adjustment (2,150 − 1,200 − 65)	(885) Environmental provision
Accumulated profit in the balance sheet	3,409

W2 Plant and machinery – change in method of depreciation

		$000	
Last year	Old method (250 − 50 = 200 × 2000/8000)	50	
	New method (250 × 20%)	50	nil
Current year	Old method (250 − 50 = 200 × 800/8000)	20	
	New method (250 − 50 = 200 × 20%)	40	20 additional deprec.

W3 Leased plant – finance lease not operating lease

	$
Total payments (10 × $75,000)	750,000
Fair value/cost	600,000
Total finance costs	150,000

	Opening balance	**Rentals paid**	**Net liability**	**Finance cost**	**Closing balance**
1.4.2001	600,000	75,000	525,000	26,000	551,000
1.10.2001	551,000	75,000	*476,000	24,000	500,000
1.4.2002	500,000	75,000	425,000	21,000	446,000
1.10.2002	446,000	75,000	371,000	19,000	390,000

Depreciation should be $600,000 \times 20\% = \$120,000$ per annum (assumed 5-year life).
The journal entries would be as follows:

Dr			
	Leased assets (600 − 120)	480	
	Interest (26 + 24)	50	
	Depreciation	120	
Cr	Finance obligations – non-current		371
	Finance obligations – current		105
			476
	Lease rentals		150
	Accrued interest		24
		650	650

W4 Convertible loan note

This is a compound loan note, and IAS 32 *Financial Instruments: Disclosure and Presentation* requires the debt instrument to be split between its debt and equity components. The amount of the issue proceeds attributable to the conversion rights is classified as equity. This is usually the residue after the value of the debt component has been calculated.

	Cash flows	Factor at 10%	Present value $000
Year 1 interest	180	0.91	164
Year 2 interest	180	0.83	149
Year 3 interest	180	0.75	135
Year 4 interest, redemption premium and capital (3,000 + 300 + 180)	3,480	0.68	2,366
Total value of debt component			2,814
Proceeds of the issue			3,000
Total equity element			186

The interest cost must be increased from $180 to $281 (10% × $2,814) by accruing an additional $101, and this should be added to the carrying amount of the debt.

W5 Proposed dividend

Market capitalisation of ordinary shares is $10m (5m × $2). A yield of 4% would require a dividend of 4% × $10m = $400,000. This is a contingency liability under IAS 10.

(b)   Calculation of Earnings Per Share

Earnings	
Profit attributable to ordinary shareholders	$1,794,000
Number of shares	
Ordinary shares issued and outstanding for the year	5m ($2.5m × 2)
Basic EPS	
$1,794,000/(5m × 100)	35.9c
Earnings	
As per basic	$1,794,000
Savings in interest (net of tax relief lost on interest paid)	
($281,000 − ($180,000 × 25%))	236,000
	$2,030,000

Number of shares
As per basic   5m
Conversion of loan notes (3m × 50/100)   1.5m
                                                                              6.5m

Diluted EPS
$2,030,000/6.5m × 100   31.2c

Solution 5.3: Company X

(a) Potential problems of placing undue emphasis on earnings per share

If undue importance is placed on the EPS figure, it is possible that this could lead to simplistic interpretations of financial performance. The accounting regulators have attempted to de-emphasise EPS by requiring it to be calculated after extraordinary items. The EPS number so calculated became a starting point for further analysis, and the regulators recognised that companies would provide additional EPS numbers on some more meaningful basis. There is a body of opinion that feels that EPS is not an appropriate subject for a standard since it deals with financial analysis rather than financial reporting.

The purpose of EPS is to allow comparability between companies. However, the earnings stated in corporate reports are not necessarily comparable with each other because of differing accounting policies and there will be different levels of earnings from non-trading transactions, which will not be representative of a company's earnings potential. Additionally, the level of taxation suffered may not be consistent between companies. Thus there may be problems if the EPS figure is used for investment purposes or as part of the Price Earnings ratio when valuing a company's shares, if the inconsistencies in corporate financial reporting are not taken into account and a wider range of information about the company is not provided.

(b) The nature of the 'reporting gap' and how it might be eliminated

Companies use news releases, meetings, road shows and conference calls to analysts and investors, as well as annual reports and other statutory channels to communicate with users. Unfortunately the results of such communications are often fragmentary, with incomplete communication occurring. Companies need, perhaps, a more structured, systematic way of communicating to users. Directors should communicate to investors and analysts the performance measures which they believe to be important in managing their companies.

The failure to do this to date has led investors and analysts to focus on earnings and cash flows because this is the type of information provided. The largest gaps in information occur in the non-financial measures, but there is reluctance on the part of directors to provide this type of information. If directors want the market to focus on longer-term value creation, then information such as new product development, market share, market growth and customer satisfaction should be provided in a 'balanced scorecard' of financial and non-financial measures of value. The reliance on the statutory reporting process and the perceived risk attached to disclosing too much information militate against the development of a more informed opinion of a company's true value.

There is a gap between the importance that directors place on the measures they use to manage the company and the communication of such to the market. The financial statements make little reference to the critical value of 'people'. There are measurement issues, but spending on training and staff turnover, and customer retention, which can be quantified, are seldom promoted to the financial markets.

The financial markets demand a 'balanced scorecard' of information about value creation in a company. Directors are not communicating this as positively as it could be.

(c) Calculation of basic and diluted Earnings Per Share for Company X for the year ended 31 May 2001

Basic Earnings Per Share

Earnings

		$000
Net profit for the year attributable to ordinary and preference shareholders		14,600
Less preference dividends: 600,000 × 6% × 1/2	18	
400,000 × 6%	24	42
Net profit available to ordinary shareholders		14,558

Number of shares

	Shares (000)	Period	Weighted average shares	
1.6.2000 to 31.8.2000	6,000	3/12	1,500	Opening shares
1.9.2000 to 1.12.2000	7,200	3/12	1,800	Full issue
1.12.2000 to 1.1.2001	7,500	1/12	625	Conversion pref. shares
1.1.2001 to 1.4.2001	7,650	3/12	1,913	Partly paid (50%)
1.4.2001 to 31.5.2001	7,800	2/12	1,300	Conversion loan
			7,138	($5m × 30/1000)

Although the warrants were exercised before the accounts were approved, there is an inflow of resources from the event and thus EPS is not adjusted for the current year.

Basic Earnings Per Share: $\dfrac{(\$14{,}558{,}000 \times 100)}{7{,}138{,}000} = \$2.04$

Diluted Earnings Per Share

			$000
Earnings			
Earnings as per basic EPS			14,558
Add interest saved on loan stock	$15m × 5%	750	
	$5m × 5% × 10/12	208	
		958	
less tax relief lost at 30%		(287)	671
preference dividend	400,000 × 6%	24	
	600,000 × 6% × 1/2	18	42
			15,271

Number of shares

As per basic	7,138
Add partly paid shares	
(consideration outstanding 300,000 × $4 = $1.2m / $10 = 120,000	
issued for no consideration 150,000 − 120,000)	30
convertible loan stock	
($20m × 30/1000 × 10/12 + $15m × 30/1000 × 2/12)	575
convertible preference shares	
($1m / 2 × 6/12 + $0.4m / 2 × 6/12)	350
warrants	
(600,000 × 34% discount ($10 − 6.60 = 3.40/10) = 204 × 5/12	85
	8,178

Diluted EPS: $\dfrac{(\$11,971,000 \times 100)}{8,178,000} = \$1.46$

Working

Calculation of anti-dilutive potential ordinary shares

	$000	Ordinary shares $000	Per share $
Profit from continuing ordinary activities less			
Preference dividend ($14,558,000 − $3.3m)	11,258	7,138	1.58
Warrants	–	85	
	11,258	7,223	1.56
Partly paid shares	–	30	
	11,258	7,253	1.55
Convertible preference shares	42	350	
	11,300	7,603	1.49
Convertible loan stock	671	575	
	11,971	8,178	1.46

All potential ordinary shares have a dilutive effect and therefore all of these shares must be included in the diluted EPS calculation. The sequencing is from the most to the least dilutive.

Presentation of basic and diluted Earnings Per Share

	Basic	Diluted
Profit from continuing operations	1.58	1.46
Profit from discontinued operations	0.56	0.12
Net profit	2.04	1.58

Solution 5.4: G

(a) Income statement and balance sheet

Income statement for G for the year ended 31 December 2000

	Notes	$m
Revenue		1,000
Cost of sales (240 − 5 pension paid + 2 pension charge)		(237)

Gross profit		763
Distribution costs (100 + 8 bad debt)	1	(108)
Administration expenses		(130)
Profit from operations		525
Interest cost		(95)
Profit before tax		430
Income tax	2	(190)
Profit on ordinary activities after tax		240
Dividends – interim		(40)
Net profit for the period		200

Balance sheet of G as at 31 December 2000

	Notes	$m	$m
Non-current assets			
Property, plant and equipment			2,400
Goodwill			1,900
			4,300
Current assets			
Inventory		110	
Trade and other receivables (90 − 8 bad debt)		82	
Prepayments (5 − 2 pensions)		3	
Bank		10	205
Total assets			4,505
Equity and liabilities			
Ordinary shares of $1 each, fully paid up (400 + 100)			500
Share premium (360 + 40)			400
Accumulated profits (1,875 + 200 retained for year)			2,075
			2,975
Non-current liabilities			
Interest bearing borrowings		1,100	
Deferred tax (200 + 80)		280	1,380
Current liabilities			
Trade and other payables		30	
Taxation		120	150
Total equity and liabilities			4,505

Notes:

1. Distribution costs
Included in distribution costs is an exceptional bad debt write-off of $8 million.

2. Taxation

	$m
Charge for year	120
Over provision in previous year	(10)
Increase in provision for deferred tax	80
	190

3. Dividends
The company has proposed a final dividend of $60 million.

4. Pensions

The company operates a pension scheme which provides benefits based on final pay. The assets of the scheme are held separately from those of the company.

	$m
Regular pension cost based on % of earnings	8
Variation from regular cost	2
Net pension cost	10
Pension payments made (8 + 5)	13

The $3 million prepaid pension cost is not recoverable within 1 year.

5. Share capital and share premium

	Share capital $m	Share premium $m
Balance at 31 December 1999	400	360
Issued during the year	100	40
Balance at 31 December 2000	500	400

6. Deferred taxation

	$m
Balance at 31 December 1999	200
Increase in provision	80
	280

7. Profit and loss account

	$m
Balance at 31 December 1999	1,875
Net profit for the period	200
	2,075

8. Post-balance sheet event

A damages claim was lodged against the company after the year end for the sum of $2 million. This matter has now been placed in the hands of the company's legal advisors, who are of the opinion that this sum will have to be paid in compensation.

(b) Calculation of Earnings Per Share

Earnings

Profits after taxation			$240m

Number of shares

| 1.1.2000 to 29.2.2000 | 400m × 2/12 | 67 | |
| 1.3.2000 to 31.12.2000 | 500m × 10/12 | 417 | 484m |

Earnings per share

$$\frac{\$240m \times 100}{484}$$ 49.6c

(c) Reasons for calculating an earnings per share figure

EPS is a crucial indicator of performance for analysts and other users, particularly as it forms the base for the price/earnings ratio (P/E ratio) that is quoted every day in the newspapers. It is therefore important that as much consistency and comparability as possible be introduced into its calculation, otherwise directors will tend to manipulate the figure to achieve their own desired performance.

(d) What is meant by 'diluted' earnings, and why should this figure be disclosed as well?

Many companies issue financial instruments which are currently in the form of loans but may become equity shares at some time in the future. One example of this is the issue of convertible debentures. These are currently debentures upon which interest must be paid each year. However, the holders of the debentures are given an option of either redemption of the debenture at some time in the future, or conversion of the debenture loan into ordinary shares. If the debenture holders do choose to convert the debentures into ordinary shares then there will be more ordinary shares in issue, and this is likely to have an effect on the EPS.

For this reason, if companies do have convertible debentures in issue then they must not only disclose the basic EPS figure but also a diluted EPS. The diluted EPS is prepared on the assumption that the debenture holders have in fact already converted their debentures into ordinary shares. In order to calculate the diluted EPS, the interest paid on the debentures is added back to increase earnings and the number of ordinary shares that the debenture holders can convert to is added to the basic number of shares in issue.

In this way, information is being given to shareholders about the effect of the potential conversion of the debentures on the EPS. A further example of capital instruments which may become shares in future are loans or debentures issued with warrants giving the right to buy ordinary shares of the company in future. These future potential shares must also be taken into account when calculating the diluted EPS.

Solution 5.5: Myriad

(a) When should a company change its accounting policies?

Included in the fundamental characteristics of financial reporting is that of consistency – i.e. similar items should be accounted for in a consistent manner from period to period and in each accounting period. Thus if a company wishes to change its accounting policy, this should only occur if a new policy is more appropriate. This usually occurs on a change in accounting standard or change in law. It also occurs on acquisitions, as subsidiaries need to draw up their statements on uniform accounting policies of the group as a whole.

(b) Extracts from financial statements for Myriad

Income statement (extract)

	30 September 2001		30 September 2000 (restated)
	$000		$000
Amortisation of development costs $(1,060 \times 25\%)$	265	$(1,060 - 400 \times 25\%)$	165

Balance sheet (extract)

Intangible non-current assets			
Development expenditure $(1,230 - 505 \text{ amortisation})$	725	$(670 - 240 \text{ amortisation})$	430

Under IAS 8 *Accounting Policies, Changes in Accounting Estimates and Errors*, the amount of the prior year adjustment would have been the 420 cost less 75 amortisation (25% × 300) = 345. This would have to be adjusted and added to the accumulated profits as at 1 October 2000.

Working

W1

Amortisation to 30 September 2000	300 × 25% × 2 years	150	
	360 × 25% × 1 year	90	240
	660		
Amortisation to 30 September 2001	300 × 25% × 3 years	225	
	360 × 25% × 2 years	180	
	400 × 25% × 1 year	100	505
	1,060		

(c)   Possible accounting treatments for investment properties

The main reasons for holding investment properties are that the owner expects to receive rental income from them as well as capital appreciation. They are not held for 'consumption' in the normal course of business – i.e. for production, administration etc. As they are held as an investment, it is argued that the current values in those properties and any changes therein are the most appropriate to adopt. IAS 40 *Investment Properties*, however, permits a choice between its benchmark 'cost' model or its allowed alternative 'fair value' model.

Cost model

Properties should be measured at depreciated historic cost and thus are treated similarly to owner occupied properties. However, fair values must be disclosed.

Fair value model

Properties should be measured at fair value with any changes recognised within the income statement.

(d)   Fair value method

Consolidated balance sheet as at 30 September 2001 (extracts)

	Cost/valuation $000	Accumulated depreciation $000	NBV $000
Non-current assets			
Property, plant and equipment – A	150	6 (2 years)	144
Investment property – B	145	nil	145
Investment property – C	150	nil	150

Consolidated income statement for the year ended 30 September 2001 (extracts)

Depreciation – property A	(3)	(150/50 years)
Deficit in fair value of investment property B (180 − 145)	(35)	
Surplus in fair value of investment property C (140 − 150)	10	

Solution 5.6: Pailing

(a) The main reasons why multinational companies might wish IAS to be adopted

1. To raise finance in a number of stock exchanges throughout the world
2. To improve comparability of financial information across borders
3. To reduce the costs of preparation of financial statements
4. To help internal management by the adoption of a common accounting language
5. To provide a reliable basis for corporate analysis
6. To improve financial transparency and reduce the practice of 'financial shopping'.

(b) The problems with IASs that may act as a barrier to their acceptance

1. Loss of national sovereignty in setting accounting standards
2. Use of 'benchmark' and 'allowed alternatives' reduces comparability
3. Significant cost in converting from national standards to IASs
4. National tax authorities may not accept IASs for tax purposes
5. Not as detailed as US or other standards – possible dilution of quality of standards
6. Need for an effective enforcement mechanism throughout the world.

(c) Restatement of net profit for the year ended 31 March 2000 and capital and reserves as at 31 March 2000

	Net profit	Capital and reserves
Net profit/balance for the year to/as at 31 March 2000	89	225
(i) *Change in accounting policy*		
Under SIC 8 no prior year adjustment – charged instead direct to income (30 − 3)	27	
(ii) *Minority interest*		
Share of net loss since acquisition (25% × 24 − 28)		(1)
Increase in net assets for the group		1
(iii) *Negative goodwill*		
Purchase consideration $16m −75% net assets $28 = $5m negative goodwill		

Reverse immediate write-off	(5)	(5)
Recognise over 5-year life of non-monetary assets	1	1
(iv) *Gain on sale*		
Should be $40 − $36m = $4m not $8m	(4)	
Under IAS 21 exchange gain recycled to income	3	
(v) *Deferred tax*		
Full provision $6m × 30% = $1.8m − $0.3m current		(1.5)
Charge for the year $13m × 30% = $3.9 − $1.8m − 0.6m (1.5)		(1.5)
current charge		
Revised net profit/balance for the year/as at 31 March 2000	109.5	218

(d)   Effect of restatement on purchase decision

Changes in accounting policy should not impact on the purchase decision. It should be neutral, as the underlying economic events have not changed. In reality that may not happen – for example, when Daimler Benz first went on to the New York Stock Exchange and prepared their accounts under US GAAP, they produced a loss of c1400Dm but recorded a profit of c600Dm in Germany. That may have a detrimental impact, as the listing in the US need not go well.

Solution 5.7: Transystems

Report to the Group Accountant *re* Acceptability of the Accounting Practices

The following discussion sets out an opinion on the acceptability of the proposed accounting practices of the Transystems group:

Acquisition of Zest Software

IFRS 3 *Business Combinations* establishes that goodwill should not be amortised. The carrying forward of goodwill at its original amount is now compulsory. Amortisation was originally charged on the straight-line basis. Under IFRS 3's transitional arrangements, goodwill should remain at its net book value and subsequently must be reviewed annually for impairment.

Interest in joint venture

The amount currently stated in the balance sheet for the joint venture can be broken down as follows:

	$m
Loan to joint venture	5
Net interest in joint venture	3
Negative goodwill	(6)
	2

There are several points to be taken into account in this matter. IAS 28 *Accounting for Investments in Associates* states that where the investors' share of losses exceeds the carrying value of the investment, then the investor discontinues including its share of further losses and the investment is reported at nil value. Thus the IAS by implication would not concur with the reporting of a negative value for a joint venture accounted for under the equity method of accounting which is dealt with by IAS 28. It would be unusual to include a loan to the joint venture as part of the net investment, as the loans are assets of the investor. By taking out and reporting the loan separately, a net liability of $3 million arises. The question arises as to whether this amount should be shown as a liability or negative asset. Negative goodwill under IFRS 3's transitional arrangements must be transferred from being presented as a deduction from the assets of the company and instead transferred back to revenue reserves.

Negative goodwill should be recognised in the income statement of the period. Previously, goodwill was only recognised in income in the period the losses occurred, or, if certain conditions set out above were not met, then negative goodwill was recognised over the weighted average useful life of the depreciable non-monetary assets (excluding land). If the value of negative goodwill exceeded the fair values of the non-monetary assets, the excess had to be recognised immediately.

Music and screen production rights/domain name

IAS 38 *Intangible Assets* states that if an intangible asset is acquired in a business combination, the cost of that intangible asset is based on its fair value at the date of acquisition assuming that it can be measured reliably. Intangible assets are shown under non-current assets, and they are subject to impairment testing and amortisation. The treatment used by Transystems avoids this, and leaves the production rights to be treated under IAS 2 *Inventories.* This means that they will be shown at the lower of historical cost and net realisable value. IAS 38 is quite convincing in its argument that the production rights should be treated as intangible assets, amortised and reviewed for impairment. In order to meet the definition of an intangible asset, IAS 38 requires identifiability, control and the existence of future economic benefits. It would appear that the domain names should be shown as an intangible asset and not as a tangible non-current asset. Further, on actual recognition, the intangible asset should be measured at cost. Any subsequent revaluation using the allowed alternative treatment is only possible if an active market exists for the intangible. The definition of an 'active market' is quite stringent to the extent that very few intangibles have such a market. Thus the domain name costs should be shown at cost under intangible assets and amortised/reviewed for impairment.

Revenue recognition on sale of software under licences

US revenue recognition rules are more advanced than IAS 18 *Revenue*, which deals with the subject. The revenue recognition policies adopted by Transystems do not contravene IAS 18, and it is normal practice in many parts of the world to adopt US GAAP if it provides further guidance on an accounting practice covered by IAS.

IAS 18 requires that accounting for a transaction should reflect its substance. If a transaction consists of distinct elements, then each element should be accounted for separately. It could be argued as regards policy (i) that where the selling price of the product includes an identifiable amount for subsequent servicing, that amount is deferred and recognised as revenue over the period during which the service is performed. The amount deferred is that which will cover the expected costs of services together with a reasonable profit on those services. However, it could instead be argued that the 'transactions' are linked and in order to properly reflect their economic substance they should be treated together. It will essentially depend on the substance and nature of the transaction.

IAS 18 *Revenue* states that fees from the development of customised software should be recognised as revenue by reference to the stage of completion of the development, including completion of services provided for post-delivery service support. Thus accounting policy (ii) should be changed to comply with IAS 18.

Property – long and short leasehold

IAS 16 *Property, Plant and Equipment* states that the cost of an asset is depreciated over its useful life. The standard requires a depreciation charge to be made even if the asset is worth more than its carrying amount. IAS 16 allows two ways of estimating residual value. The residual value must be revalued at each revaluation date. IAS 16 does not say that depreciation does not have to be charged where the asset has a long life or the amount is not material. Also, if the long leasehold properties are held to the end of their lease term then their residual value will be very low, hence it would seem that the company must intend selling the properties before this date in order for their residual values to be so high. If this is not the case, then the view of the company that the long leasehold properties have high residual values must be looked at with a degree of scepticism. Thus to avoid depreciating the long leasehold property the asset must be revalued at each balance sheet date, whereupon its value should not have fallen from the previous revalued amount. It has been argued that depreciation may be avoided because an enterprise will maintain the asset such that its fair value is maintained at a level similar to that at which it was purchased. The argument fails because the effect of maintaining an asset is to increase its economic life and at the end of its economic life the asset's residual value will be unaffected.

The policy for short leasehold properties is not in line with IAS 16, which states that the depreciation charge should be made throughout the asset's useful economic life and not just towards the end of its life. The current practice adopted by the company of non-depreciation and re-negotiation appears to be a deliberate attempt to avoid depreciating the short leasehold properties.

Boxed presentation and multi-column formats

With the need to highlight information in the income statement, an increasingly popular way of doing this is through the use of a boxed presentation. Companies have complete freedom as to how they use boxed presentations, and companies which do so utilise box presentation for a diverse range of subjects. Thus there is no problem in using boxed presentations as long as they are not used in excess, as they may be a source of confusion if they are overused. Additionally, boxed presentations may be used as a distraction in order to de-emphasise possibly poor results. For example, if gross margins are good these may attract a boxed format whilst poor net profit may not be 'boxed'.

Solution 5.8: Sandown

(a)   Definition of a discontinuing operation

A discontinuing operation is a relatively large component of an entity that, pursuant to a single co-ordinated plan, is:

- being disposed of substantially in its entirety;
- being sold off on a piecemeal basis; or
- being terminated.

It must represent a major line of business (either product or geographical) and must be distinguished operationally and for reporting purposes. It usually equates, in a large business, to the segments defined in IAS 14 *Segment Reporting*.

There must be an intention to dispose of the entirety of the operation even if it is not in a single transaction, and the 'plan' should be formal and identify:

- the part of the business concerned;
- the principal locations and number of employees concerned; and
- the expenditures and timings of closure.

The planned closure must lead to a constructive obligation by raising a valid expectation in those affected by the decision that the plan will be implemented. Thus under IAS 35 *Discontinuing Operations* there must be an initial disclosure of the event, i.e. the earlier of the point where a binding sale agreement is entered into or the detailed plan is approved and announced. This is not necessarily the same time as the actual closure or sale, which may take several years to achieve.

If the initial event occurs after the year end but before the accounts are approved, then information relating to that discontinuance should be included in the current year's financial statements. Comparatives for prior periods must be restated to ensure comparability for the purpose of trend information. IAS 35 has been superseded by IFRS 5 *Non-Current Assets Held For Sale and Presentation of Discontinued Operations*, but the definition has not changed significantly. However, discontinued operations must be presented as a single amount on the profit and loss account, but after the profit on continuing operations.

(b)   The benefits to users of providing discontinuing operations information

More emphasis is being placed on the future than on the past in financial reporting, and clearly information on discontinuing operations should be eliminated in order to get a better view of the likely future trend of performance.

An important element of this is the presentation of restated figures for continuing operations in prior years. This enables a more like to like comparison being made from year to year.

(c) Sandown – revised income statement (under IFRS 5)

	Year ended 30.9.2001	Year ended 30.9.2002
	$m	**$m**
Sales revenue	920	850
Cost of sales	(600)	(530)
Gross profit	320	320
Operating expenses	(80)	(120)
Profit for the period from continuing operations	240	200
Loss from discontinued operations	(110)	(50)
Profit for the period	130	150

(d) Closure costs of website

IAS 35 does not provide guidance on how to calculate the provision for closure costs. This is left up to a more specific accounting standard, IAS 37 *Provisions, Contingent Liabilities and Contingent Assets*.

The general requirement in IAS 37 is that only the direct expenditures arising from a closure be provided for. The direct expenditures must be both necessary and not associated with the ongoing activities of the entity. By applying this logic it would mean that staff retraining costs of $12m and future operating losses of $28m could not be provided for in 2001 unless the losses relate to an onerous contract. They should be charged to income in the period they are incurred.

Solution 5.9: Rationalise

(a) Income statement of Rationalise for the year ended 30 September 2000

	$
Revenue	893,000
Cost of sales	(578,000)
Gross profit	315,000
Operating expenses	(151,100)
Depreciation (*W2*)	(20,000)
Operating profit/(loss)	143,900
Interest (1,900 + 15,000 preference dividend)	(16,900)
Profit/(loss) before tax	127,000
Income tax (*W5*)	(33,300)
Profit for the period from continuing operations	93,700
Loss for the period from discontinued operations	(36,200)
Income tax	7,500
Profit after tax	65,000

(b) Balance sheet of Rationalise as at 30 September 2000

	$	$
Non-current assets		
Property, plant and equipment (*W2*)		630,500

Current assets		
Inventories (160 + 65)	225,000	
Trade receivables (244.2 + 108.7)	352,900	
Bank	16,000	593,900
Total assets		1,224,400
Capital and reserves		
Equity shares of 25c each		500,000
Reserves		
Revaluation (20 − 6 *W5*)	14,000	
Accumulated profits (90 + 65 − 10)	145,000	159,000
		659,000
Non-current liabilities		
Deferred tax (*W5*)	12,000	
10% preference shares	150,000	162,000
Current liabilities		
Bank overdraft (33.1 − 12 cash in transit)	21,100	
Trade payables (136.9 + 193.9)	330,800	
Taxation	19,000	
Proposed dividends (7.5)	7,500	
Provision for closure costs	25,000	403,400
Total equity and liabilities		1,224,400

Working

W1 Cost of sales

	Head Office	**Branch**
	$	**$**
Opening inventories	136,100	53,400
Manufacturing expenses	545,900	461,600
Depreciation (*W2*)	56,000	16,000
Closing inventories (*W4*)	(160,000)	(65,000)
	578,000	466,000

W2 Non-current assets and depreciation

	Head Office	**Branch**
Depreciation		
Buildings 2% × $300,000	6,000	
Plant 20% × $250,000	50,000	16,000 20% × $80,000
	56,000	16,000
Motor vehicles 25% × ($170 − 90)	20,000	7,500 25% × ($45 − 15)

Property, plant and equipment	**Cost**	**Depreciation**	**NBV**
Land and buildings (210 + 300)	510	(80 + 6) 86	424
Plant and equipment (250 + 80)	330	(110 + 30 + 50 + 16) 206	124
Motor vehicles (170 + 45)	215	(90 + 15 + 20 + 7.5) 132.5	82.5
	1,055	424.5	630.5

W3 Costs of closure

Only direct costs of the closure can be provided for. IAS 37 *Provisions, Contingent Liabilities and Contingent Assets* disallows the inclusion foreseeable losses from being included as part of closure costs unless they relate to an onerous contract.

W4   Closing inventory

Head office		164,000
Less damaged inventory write-down		
(80% × 25,000 = 20,000 − 6,000 − (10% × 20,000))	12,000 NRV	
	16,000 Cost	(4,000)
		160,000

W5   Income tax

Head office	32,500
Deferred tax	6,000 (20,000 plant × 30%)
Over provision in 1999	(5,200)
	33,300

Deferred tax on buildings 20,000 × 30% = 6,000 should be charged to the revaluation reserve.

W6   Current accounts

Branch current account 81,500 − Head Office accounts 69,500 = 12,000 cash in transit.

W7   Dividends

Equity dividends – interim	10,000	Charged to reserves
– final (2m × 1 c)	20,000	Contingent liability
Preference – interim 7,500 + final 7,500		15,000
(included as interest payable)		

Solution 5.10: Halogen

(a)   Balance sheet of Halogen as at 31 March 2001

	$ million	$ million
Non-current assets		
Property, plant and equipment (910 + 330 + 10 + 8)		1,258
Goodwill (150 − 30 *W2*)		120
Development expenditure (100 − 8 *W1*)		92
Investments (700 − 480 *W2* + 60)		280
		1,750
Current assets		
Inventories (224 + 120 − 3 *W1*)	341	
Trade receivables (264 + 84 − 12 in transit)	336	
Bank	25	702
Total assets		2,452
Equity and liabilities		
Capital and reserves		
Equity shares of $1 each		1,000
Share premium	300	
Accumulated profits (*W1*)	486	
Revaluation reserve (*W5*)	76	
		862
		1,862
Minority interest (W3)		120

Non-current liabilities
10% Debenture   60

Current liabilities
Bank overdraft	(86 − 12 in transit)	74
Trade payables	(128 + 24)	152
Creditor – minority interest	(25% × 20)	5
Taxation	(94 + 35)	129
Proposed dividends		50
		410

Total equity and liabilities   2,452

Working

W1   Accumulated profits

Unrealised profit on inventory	3	Balance – Halogen	480
Unrealised profit in development	28	Balance – Stimulus	240
Minority interest (25% × (240 − 28))	53	Dividend from Stimulus	15
Cost of control (75% × 180)	135	(75% × 20)	
Goodwill amortised (*W3*)	30		
Consolidated B/S	486		
	735		735

Unrealised profit on development is its transfer value of $36m less book value of $8m.
Unrealised profit on inventory (26 × 30/130 × 50% unsold) = $3m.

W2   Cost of control

Investment at cost	480	Equity shares (75% × 200)	150
(200m × 75%/2 × $5)	= 375	Acc. profits (75% × 180)	135
(cash paid 200m × 75%/2 × $1.40) =	105	Fair value adjustments	15
		Revaluation reserve (75% × 40)	30
		Goodwill	150
	480		480

Goodwill of $150m is amortised over 5-year life = $30m per annum.

W3   Minority interest

Consolidated B/S	120	Equity shares (25% × 200)	50
		Accumulated profits	53
		Fair value adjustments	5
		Revaluation reserve (*W5*)	12
	120		120

W4   Fair value adjustments

Minority interest (25%)	5	Development exp (28 − 8)	20
Cost of control (75%)	15		
	20		20

W5   Revaluation reserve

Minority interest (25% × 48)	12	Balance – Halogen	60
Cost of control (75% × 40)	30	Balance – Stimulus	40
Consolidated B/S	76	Surplus – Halogen	10
		Surplus – Stimulus	8
	118		118

(b)   Suitability of the accounting treatment for Lockstart

The advantage in preparing an income statement that concentrates on 'current operating income' is that it reports the results of those parts of a business that can be expected to be operating in the future, and this forms a useful basis from which to predict the future income streams of the company. However, the accounting profession has rejected this, mainly because it would lead to incomplete reporting and the introduction of greater subjectivity and to reporting selectively only certain aspects of performance. The directors of Halogen are partly correct in interpreting IFRS 5 *Non-Current Assets Held For Sale and Presentation of Discontinued Operations* in that by identifying and separately reporting discontinuing operations this helps the predictive process. However, IFRS 5 does not permit the omission of the results of those parts of the business that have been or are about to be discontinued.

IAS 27 *Consolidated Financial Statements and Accounting for Investment in Subsidiaries* requires subsidiaries that are held exclusively for resale in the near future to be excluded from consolidation. Instead they should be recorded as a current asset. Exclusion from consolidation is only available for subsidiaries that have never previously been consolidated. In practice, this exemption is mainly used where a group has been acquired and some of the activities of some of the subsidiaries within the acquired group do not form part of the acquiring group's future plans. The intention is therefore to dispose of them as quickly as possible. In the case of Lockstart exclusion would not be possible, but under IFRS 5, provided the future disposal meets the criteria in IFRS 5 to be reported as discontinuing, it may be presented as such in the income statement. Thus the directors' treatment of excluding Lockstart from consolidation is incorrect and they should be advised to redraft the accounts to include its results, possibly as part of discontinuing operations, and there may be a need further provisions for some of the future costs associated with the disposal.

Solution 5.11: Desolve

Effects of events relating to the closure of the subsidiary on the financial statements of Desolve

When a company decides to discontinue an operation, it has to investigate a number of accounting standards when deciding on the appropriate accounting treatment. These are:

- IFRS 5 *Non-Current Assets Held For Sale and the Presentation of Discontinued Operations;*
- IAS 37 *Provisions, Contingent Liabilities and Contingent Assets;*
- IAS 19 *Employee Benefits;* and
- IAS 36 *Impairment of Assets.*

As a result, the accounting treatment can be quite complex as the standards interplay with each other.

IFRS 5

As the plan to discontinue a major component of the business has been approved by the board of directors and publicly announced to those affected, Desolve should recognise the results of the discontinued operation, including any gain/loss on realisation as a separate section of the income statement, recorded below profit from continuing operations. At the same time, it must recognise any impairment losses, restructuring provisions etc. arising from the plan.

A discontinued operation must be a component of an entity that has either been disposed of or is classified as 'held for sale' and:

- represents a separate major line of business or geographical area of operations; or
- is part of a single coordinated plan to dispose of a separate major line of business or geographical area of operations; or
- is a subsidiary acquired exclusively with a view to resale.

This is clearly the case here.

An entity shall disclose a single amount on the face of the Profit and Loss comprising the post-tax profit/loss of discontinued operations and the post-tax gains/losses on measurement to fair value or on disposal of discontinued operations. Further analysis is required in the notes *re* revenue, expenses and pre-tax profits/losses of discontinued operations, as well as the net cash flows attributable to the operating, investing and financing activities of discontinued operations.

IAS 37

Before a restructuring provision may be created, Desolve must identify the principal locations and functions, the approximate numbers of employees to be terminated, the expenditure, and when the plan will be implemented.

A provision for the closure of the operations is also governed by IAS 37. The closure is a discontinuing decision under IFRS 5, but the measurement and recognition rules are in IAS 37. IAS 37 also requires a detailed formal plan and a valid expectation that the plan will be effected by those employees affected. The expenditure to be provided is restricted to direct expenditure only and is not associated with the ongoing operations of the company. Future losses, however, may not be provided for.

A provision of $15m for closing the glass-making operation should be provided for, as well as the $3m potential profit which has to added back to give $18m as the 'true' cost of discontinuing. This should not have been included in non-current assets but instead fully expensed in income as well as creating a non-current liability. The operating losses of $20m cannot be provided, as they could be avoided if the operation was shutdown immediately. The costs of retraining staff and relocating them is not permitted either. These are regarded as normal ongoing costs which should be charged when incurred. They are not legal or constructive obligations.

IAS 19

The company has agreed to pay its employees redundancy pay under a termination and redundancy agreement. A formal plan has been drawn up and communicated to the employees on 30 June 2001; thus a legal obligation has been created by the year end and must be provided for. As this is a voluntary agreement, the company must make their best estimate of the likely cost of payment. As 75% of the employees are expected to take up the offer, this should cost the company 75% × $80m = $60m. Normally that should be provided, but before the accounts were approved the actual payment turned out to be only $56m. This constitutes an adjusting event, as it does provide additional evidence of conditions existing at the balance sheet date under IAS 10 *Events After The Balance Sheet Date*, and so the final liability should only be $56m on the balance sheet.

The redundancy creates what is termed a 'curtailment without a settlement' under IAS 19 for the defined benefit pension plan. This reduces the net present value of the obligation by $50m, which should reduce the amount recorded as a liability on the balance sheet. The fair value of the assets in the scheme is unaffected by the decision to curtail activities, but there is effectively a gain on settlement of $50m which can be recorded in the income statement, as the company is demonstrably committed to reducing the employees covered by the plan as at that date.

IAS 36

IAS 36 contains the rules as to how to calculate an impairment on assets and how it might be allocated across the various assets affected. The equipment currently has a net book value of $10m but a recoverable amount of only $8m (being the higher of NPV $7m and NRV $8m). There is evidence in the post-balance sheet period that the asset was sold eventually for $6m, but that added to the cash flows of $7m during the period to November 2001 suggests a possible NPV of $13m, which means that no impairment has taken place.

The trade receivable of $8m clearly exists at the year end. The directors have no legal obligation to pay the trade receivable as that party is not a creditor and thus any legal action by that party is likely to fail. The only likely liability would be a guarantee by Desolve to support the trade receivable, and thus Assess could sue on those terms. More important is the likelihood of recovery of the $8m from the trade receivable, which must now be considered extremely doubtful and should be provided for in full.

Solution 5.12: Zetec Group

Consolidated income statement and balance sheet

Consolidated balance sheet as at 31 October 2001

	$m
Non-current assets (180 + 95 + 12.8 revaluation)	288
Intangible assets (0 + 2.3)	2
Goodwill (*W1*)	9
Net current assets (146 + 29 − 3 inter-co. stock profits)	172
	471
Equity and liabilities	
Ordinary shares of $1 each	65
Share premium	70
Accumulated profits (*W2*)	170
	305
Minority interest (*W3*)	12
Non current liabilities (74 + 80)	154
	471

Consolidated income statement for the year ended 31 October 2001

		$m
Revenue	(325 + 50 − 15 inter-co.)	360
Cost of sales	(189 + 25.2 − 15 + 3 goodwill + 3 stock pfts)	(205)
Gross profit		155
Distribution and administration expenses (84 + 9.2)		(93)
Interest payable (2 + 4)		(6)
Profit before taxation		56
Income tax	(15 + 6)	(21)
Profit on ordinary activities after taxation		35
Minority interest (20% × 5.6)		(1)
Retained profit for the year		34

Working

W1   Cost of control (80%)

	$m			$m
Investment in Aztec	44	Ordinary shares	(80% × 48/6)	6.4
		Share premium	(80% × 18/6)	2.4
		Revaluation reserve	(80% × 12/6)	1.6
		Accumulated profits		
			(80% × 98 − 13 research/6)	11.4
		Fair value adjs	(80% × 12.8)	10.2
		Consolidated B/S		12
	44			44

W2   Accumulated profits

	$m		$m
Cost of control	11.4	Balance – Zetec	161
Minority interest (20% × 33.3)	6.6	Balance – Aztec (*W4*)	33.3
Inter-co. stock profits			
(20% × $15)	3.0		
Goodwill amortised	3.0		
Consolidated B/S	170.3		
	194.3		194.3

W3   Minority interest (20%)

	$m			$m
Consolidated B/S	11.8	Ordinary shares	(20% × 48/6)	1.6
		Share premium	(20% × 18/6)	0.6
		Revaluation reserve	(20% × 12/6)	0.4
		Accumulated profits	(20% × 33.3)	6.6
		Fair value adjs	(20% × 12.8)	2.6
	11.8			11.8

W4   Translation of Aztec from krams into dollars – balance sheet

	Kr	Revaluation	Acc. Policy	Total	Rate	$m
Non-current assets	380			380	4	95
Intangible assets	12	(3) a		9	4	2.3
Net current assets	116			116	4	29
Long-term accounts	(320)			(320)	4	(80)
Net assets	188			185		46.3
Ordinary shares	48			48	6	8
Share premium	18			18	6	3
Revaluation reserve	12			12	6	2
Accumulated profits – pre	98		(13) c	85	6	14.2
– post	12	(3) b	13 c	22	Bal	19.1
	188			185		46.3

(a) The 'market shares' under intangible assets constitutes goodwill and should be written off over 4 years against post-acquisition profits.

(b) The amount written off the carrying value of the non-current asset is caused by a consumption of economic benefits, and the whole deficit should remain in the income statement (IAS 36 *Impairment of Assets*) unless the asset is carried at revalued amount under another IAS. Any impairment loss of a revalued asset is recognised directly against any revaluation surplus and any excess charged against the income statement (IAS 16 *Property, Plant and Equipment*). Post-acquisition reserves will be affected by the write-off against revaluation reserves. The damage had not occurred at the date of acquisition, and therefore it should not affect the calculation of goodwill.

(c) Changes in accounting policy under the benchmark treatment should be treated as a prior period adjustment and charged against opening reserves. Thus Kr13 million should be written off pre-acquisition profits and added to post-acquisition reserves. It should be eliminated from the income statement. This would bring Aztec's accounting policies into line with the IAS benchmark treatment.

W5   Fair value adjustments on acquisition of Aztec

	$m
Fair value of assets (as given) $240/6	40
Book value of assets at acquisition (8 shares + 3 premium + 2 revaluation reserves + 14.2 profits)	27.2
Fair value adjustment	12.8

W6   Inter-company stock profits

Inter-company profit is eliminated at the date the goods are passed to Aztec, i.e. $15m × 20% = $3m.

W7   Translation of Aztec's income statement from krams into dollars

	Aztec Kr	Rate	Total $m
Revenue	250	5	50
Cost of sales	(126)	5	(25.2)
Gross profit	124		24.8

Distribution and administration expenses	(46)	5	(9.2)
Interest payable	(20)	5	(4)
Taxation	(30)	5	(6)
	28		5.6
Minority interest		(20%)	(1.1)
			4.5

NB. Cost of sales in Aztec is $120 + \text{w/off}$ market share $3 + \text{w/off}$ non-current asset $3 = 126$.

The extraordinary item has been eliminated by transferring the amount relating to the damaged fixed asset (Kr3m) to cost of sales and revaluation reserve (Kr6m), and by charging opening reserves with the catch-up adjustment of Kr13 million. The transfer to revaluation reserve will leave a debit balance on the reserve when the other consolidation adjustments have been made. This balance will be transferred to consolidated reserves and minority interests.

6

Cash flow statements – solutions

Solution 6.1: Sundown

(a) Cash flow statement for the year ended 30 September 2002

		$ million	$ million
Net cash inflow from operating activities			35
Cash flows from investing activities			
Purchase of property, plant and equipment	(*W1*)	(116)	
Proceeds on sale of plant		<u>48</u>	
			(68)
Cash flows from financing activities			
Issue of ordinary shares	(*W4*)	30	
Redemption of preference shares	((50 − 0) × 110%)	<u>(22)</u>	
			<u>8</u>
Net decrease in cash and cash equivalents	(13 + 12)		<u>(25)</u>

Reconciliation of operating profit to net cash inflow from operating activities

	$ million	$ million
Profit from operations		142
Adjustments		
Depreciation on property, plant and equipment (*W1*)	45	
Loss on disposal of plant (60 − 48)	12	
Insurance claim not yet received	(15)	42
Increase in inventories (86 − 72)	(14)	
Increase in accounts receivable (74 − 41)	(33)	
Increase in accounts payable (74 − 65)	<u>9</u>	<u>(38)</u>
		146
Interest paid		(6)
Income tax paid (*W2*)		(51)
Dividends paid (*W3*)		<u>(54)</u>
		<u>35</u>

Working

W1 Property, plant and equipment

	$000		$000
Opening balance	455	Depreciation for year	45
Revaluation surplus $(40 - (15 - 4))$	29	Disposal at NBV	60
Cash – additions (bal. fig.)	116	Closing balance	495
	600		600

W2 Income tax

	$000		$000
Cash (bal. fig.)	51	Opening balance $(32 + 32)$	64
Closing balance $(40 + 21)$	61	Profit and loss	48
	112		112

W3 Dividends paid (accumulated profits)

	$000		$000
Cash (bal. fig. – dividends)	54	Opening balance – acc. profits	256
		Net profit for the period	88
Closing balance – acc. profits	294	Transfer – realised rev. reserves	4
	348		348

W4 Issue of ordinary shares

	$000		$000
Premium on preference shares		Opening balance	
charged to share premium		$(100 + 30)$	130
$((50 - 30) \times 10\%)$	2	Cash – proceeds	30
Closing balance $(120 + 38)$	158		
	160		160

W5 Movement in revaluation reserve

	$000		$000
Transfer to realised profits	4	Opening balance	15
Closing balance	40	Revaluation – year	29
	44		44

(b) Additional disclosures

IAS 7 *Cash Flow Statements* is intended to help users gain a better understanding of the financial position and liquidity of the reporting entity. The standard encourages cash flows from operations to be separated between cash flows that maintain capacity and those that increase capacity. The information permits users to assess whether the company is investing adequately in maintaining operating capacity; if not, the future performance may be impaired.

IAS 7 also encourages the separate disclosure of segment cash flow information. This disclosure is consistent with the provision of segment information within the income statement and balance sheet. In order to achieve a better understanding of the cash flows as a whole, it is useful to analyse the cash flows of its individual parts. Management needs to know which parts are producing positive cash flows and which are consuming them.

Solution 6.2: Charmer

Cash flow statement for the year ended 30 September 2001

	$ million	$ million
Net cash inflow from operating activities		635
Cash flows from investing activities		
Purchase of property, plant and equipment (*W1*)	(898)	
Purchase of non-current investments	(690)	
Investment income	120	
Proceeds of government grant (*W2*)	175	
Proceeds on sale of plant (*W1*)	170	
		(1,123)
Cash flows from financing activities		
Issue of ordinary shares (*W3*)		300
Net decrease in cash and cash equivalents		(188)

(bank (122) + (136)) = (258) + Treasury bills (120 − 50) = (188).

Reconciliation of operating profit to net cash inflow from operating activities

	$ million	$ million
Profit from operations (3,198 − 1,479)		1,719
Adjustments		
Depreciation on property, plant and equipment (80 + 276) (*W1*)	356	
Loss on disposal of plant (*W1*)	86	
Amortisation of government grants	(125)	
Negligence claim previously provided	(120)	
Increase in inventories (1,046 − 785)	(261)	
Increase in accounts receivable (935 − 824)	(111)	
Decrease in accounts payable (760 − 644)	(116)	(291)
		1,428
Interest paid (260 + 25 − 40)		(245)
Income tax paid (*W4*)		(368)
Dividends paid (30 + 150 interim (500 − 350))		(180)
		635

Working

W1 Property, plant and equipment

	$000		$000
Opening balance (land & buildings)	1,800	Disposal	500
Opening balance (plant)	1,220	Closing balance	2,000
		(land & buildings)	
Revaluation surplus (land)	150		
Purchases (balance cash additions)	898	Closing balance (plant)	1,568
	4,068		4,068

Depreciation: – property	(760 − 680)	80
– plant	(464 − (432 − 244 sold))	276

Proceeds on sale of plant (500 cost − 244 acc. depr. = 256 NBV − 86 loss = 170).

W2 Government grants

	$000		$000
Amortisation (cost of sales)	125	Opening balance (200 + 125)	325
Closing balance (275 + 100)	375	Balance (cash received)	175
	500		500

W3 Share capital

	$000		$000
Closing balance – share capital	1,400	Opening balance – share capital	1,000
Closing balance – share premium	460	Opening balance – share premium	60
		Bonus issue (1 for 10)	100
		Conversion of loan stock	
		(400 × 25/100 = 100 × 4)	400
		(100 share capital + 300 premium)	
		Balance (cash issue)	300
	1,860		1,860

W4 Share premium

	$000		$000
Closing balance	460	Opening balance	60
		Loan stock	300
		Placement	100
	460		460

W5 Share capital

	$000		$000
Closing balance	1,400	Opening balance	1,000
		Loan stock	100
		Bonus	100
		Placement	200
	1,400		1,400

W6 Income tax

	$000		**$000**
Closing balance (480 + 439)	919	Opening balance (400 + 367)	767
Cash paid (bal. fig.)	368	Income statement	520
	1,287		1,287

Solution 6.3: Squire

Cash flow statement for the year ended 31 May 2002

	$ million	**$ million**
Net cash inflow from operating activities		521
Cash flows from investing activities		
Purchase of property, plant and equipment (*W1*)	(451)	
Acquisition of subsidiary (200 + 30 onerous)	(230)	
Dividends from associates (*W3*)	50	(631)
Cash flows from financing activities		
Issue of ordinary shares (30 + 30)	60	
Repayment of long-term borrowings (1,320 − 1,270)	(50)	
Dividends paid	(85)	
Dividends paid to minority interests (*W2*)	(5)	(80)
Net decrease in cash and cash equivalents (280 − 90)		(190)

Reconciliation of operating profit to net cash inflow from operating activities

	$ million	**$ million**
Net profit before taxation		415
Adjustments		
Depreciation on property, plant and equipment	129	
Amortisation of goodwill (*W2*)	25	
Exchange difference on non-current assets	9	
Retirement benefit expense	20	
Share of operating profit in associate	(65)	
Interest payable	75	
Decrease in inventories (1,300 − (1,160 + 180 acq.)	40	
Increase in trade receivables (1,220 − 1,060)	(160)	
Increase in trade payables (2,355 − 2,105)	250	323
		738
Interest paid (*W5*)	(51)	
Income tax paid (*W4*)	(140)	
Retirement benefits paid	(26)	
		(217)
		521

Working

W1 Property, plant and equipment

	$000		$000
Opening balance	2,010	Impairment losses	194
Acquisition – Hunsten	150	Depreciation	129
Purchases (bal. fig.)	793	Closing balance	2,630
	2,953		2,953

Cash paid is purchases of $793m plus exchange difference of £9m less $351 still owed, equals $451m.

W2 Acquisition of Hungsten

	$000		$000
Purchase consideration (200 + 50)	250	Share of net assets acquired	210
		(300 × 70%)	
		Goodwill	40
	250		250

Goodwill:

	$000		$000
Opening balance	65	Amortisation (bal. fig.)	25
Acquisition of Hungsten	40	Closing balance	80
	105		105

Minority interest:

	$000		$000
Dividend paid (bal. fig.)	5	Opening balance	345
Closing balance	522	Acq. of Hungsten	
		(30% × 300)	90
		Profit for year	92
	527		527

W3 Associates

Investment in associate:

	$000		$000
Opening balance	550	Foreign exchange loss	10
Profit for the year (65 − 20 tax)	45	Dividends received	
		(bal. fig.)	50
		Closing balance	535
	595		595

W4 Income taxes

	$000		$000
Tax paid (bal. fig.)	140	Opening balance	335
		(160 + 175)	
Closing balance (200 + 200)	400	Income for year (225 − 20)	205
	540		540

W5 Interest paid

	Interest payable:		
	$000		**$000**
Unwinding of discount	4	Opening balance	45
Cash paid (bal. fig.)	51	Income statement	75
Closing balance	65		
	120		120

7

Foreign trading – solutions

Solution 7.1: Shott

(a) Financial statements and choice of method of translation

(i) Should Hammer be translated under the temporal or closing rate method of translation?

IAS 21 *The Effects of Changes in Foreign Exchange Rates* requires that entities choose the method to be used for translation so as to reflect the financial and other operational relationships between the holding company and the foreign enterprise. Mainly, this should involve the adoption of the closing rate method. The transactions are translated as if they were those of an independent entity whose cash flows are independent from those of the investor company. On the other hand, where the operations have a direct impact on those of the investing company, where the functioning of the entity is dependent on the investing company, where the currency used is mainly that of the investing company and where the major currency to which the entity is exposed is that of the investor company, then the 'integral operations' method should be adopted.

(ii) The choice of method of translation

In deciding which method to adopt, there is no single factor upon which to make the decision. In the particular case of Hammer, there are inter-company transactions – e.g. sale of goods – but only on a limited basis. The management is organised locally, its prices are determined locally, and sales are to local companies. There seems to be only limited dependence on the parent company, thus it would appear that the closing rate method would be the most appropriate method to adopt in practice.

The main purpose of translating foreign subsidiaries is to publish results that are compatible with the effects of rate changes and reflect the relationship between the two companies. Whichever method is adopted should reflect economic reality. The objectives are deemed to be as follows:

1. The preservation of the integrity of historic cost accounting
2. The presentation of the statements of a group as if they were a single economic entity
3. The presentation of information compatible with economic exposure
4. The preservation of the relationships in the original foreign currency statements
5. The choice of a consistent measurement unit.

(b) Explanation of how exchange differences are dealt with under IAS 21

Dividend

The dividend should be recorded in Shott's records at the rate ruling when the dividend was declared – i.e. at 30 September 2000:

400,000 shares $\times$ 0.15 dinars per share $\times$ 1/1.1 = $54,545

An exchange difference will arise when it is finally received in January. Shott will receive 400,000 $\times$ 0.15 $\times$ 1/1.2 = $50,000, and therefore a loss of $4,545 will need to be recorded in Shott's income statement.

The dividend paid in Hammer's accounts will be 400,000 $\times$ 0.15 $\times$ 1/ 1.44 = $41,667 – i.e. reflected at average rate. The difference between the two companies of $8,333 ($50,000 $-$ 41,667) should be treated as a movement on reserves.

Inter-company sales

The goods received from Hammer should be recorded at the date that the risks and rewards of ownership pass to Shott – i.e. 24,000 dinars $\times$ 1/1.2 = $20,000. The profit made on the transaction will be $20,000 $\times$ 25/125 = $4,000, which should be eliminated from both inventory and group profit. A gain of $5,000 would be recorded on settlement, i.e. $20,000 $-$ (24,000 dinars $\times$ 1/1.6 = $15,000), and this should be reported in the income statement of the holding company and also within the group accounts.

Loan

Where inter-company loans are deemed to be permanent, such loans should be treated as part of the net investment in the foreign company and exchange differences dealt with as adjustments to reserves. The loan would be restated at 150,000 dinars $\times$ 1/1.5, i.e. $100,000 in Shott's balance sheet. At 31 May 2001 it would be stated at 150,000 dinars $\times$ 1/1.6, i.e. $93,750 in Hammer's books with the exchange difference of $6,250 being taken to reserves.

Disposal of subsidiary

Net assets of Hammer as at 31 May 2001 is:

	Dinars (000)
Share capital	400
Profit (80,000 + 120,000)	200
	600

This is included in the consolidated accounts at 600,000 dinars $\times$ 1/1.6, i.e. $375,000 less the inter-company profit included in inventory $4,000 = $371,000.

The sale proceeds at 1 June 2001 were 825,000 dinars $\times$ 1/1.65 = $500,000, thus a profit of $129,000 should be shown in the consolidated income statement for the year ended 31 May 2002.

On the disposal of a foreign entity, the cumulative amount of exchange differences which have been deferred should be recognised as income or expenses in the same period in which the gain or loss on disposal is recognised.

Solution 7.2: Leisure

(a) Factors to consider in determining the most appropriate method of foreign currency translation

The most appropriate method of translating the results of an overseas subsidiary depends on the relationship between the parent and the subsidiary. There are two possibilities. The subsidiary is held mainly for its investment potential and conducts its operations largely independently of the parent. This means that the subsidiary enters into transactions in the local currency and is not dependent on the reporting currency of the parent. The closing rate method should be used in these circumstances. If the subsidiary is an extension of the operations of the parent (for example, the subsidiary acts as a selling agency for the parent or manufactures parts which the parent incorporates into its own products). Then this means that the transactions of the subsidiary are effectively undertaken by the parent. The temporal method is the method used to translate individual transactions, and it is appropriate in these circumstances. Under revised IAS 21, such entities must be recorded in the financial statements using the functional currency – which may be sterling even though the entity is domiciled in another country.

(b) Discuss the effects of hyperinflation on financial statements

Hyperinflation reduces the usefulness of financial statements in the following ways:

1. The amounts at which assets are stated in the balance sheet are unlikely to reflect their current values.
2. The level of profit for the year may be misleading. Income appears to increase rapidly, while expenses such as depreciation may be based on out-of-date costs and are artificially low.

It is therefore difficult to make any meaningful assessment of an entity's performance, as assets are understated and profits are overstated.

These are well-known disadvantages of basing financial statements on historic cost, and they affect most entities. However, where there is hyperinflation these problems are exacerbated.

How hyperinflation should be dealt with in the financial statements

IAS 29 *Financial Reporting in Hyperinflationary Economies* does not provide a definition of hyperinflation. However, it does include guidance as to characteristics of an economic environment of a country in which hyperinflation may be present. These include, but are not limited to, the following:

- the general population prefers to keep its wealth in non-monetary assets or in a relatively stable foreign currency;
- interest rates, wages and prices are linked to a price index;
- the cumulative inflation rate over 3 years is approaching, or exceeds, 100%.

IAS 29 states that the financial statements of an enterprise that reports in the currency of a hyperinflationary economy should be restated in terms of the measuring unit current at the balance sheet date. This involves remeasuring assets and liabilities by applying a general price index. The gain or loss on the net monetary position is included in net income and separately disclosed. The fact that the financial statements have been restated should also be disclosed, together with details of the index used.

IAS 21 *The Effects of Changes in Foreign Exchange Rates* states that where there is hyperinflation, the financial statements of a foreign operation should be restated in accordance with the requirements of IAS 29 before they are translated into the currency of the reporting enterprise. In this way users are made aware of the effect of hyperinflation on the results and net assets of the enterprise.

(c)   Using the closing rate method – carrying value of the hotel complex at 31 December 2000

(i)   Assuming the economy of Urep is not a hyperinflationary economy

The closing rate method is used. This produces a value of 50 million/220 = $227,273.

Use of the closing rate method without adjustments produces an amount based on the original cost. Because the exchange rate has increased from 25 to 220 over the life of the complex, there is a cumulative exchange loss of $1,772,727 ((50 million/25) − 227,273). The hotel complex appears to be worth much less at 31 December 2000 than when it was first acquired.

(ii)   Assuming the economy of Urep is a hyperinflationary economy

Before the cost of the hotel complex is translated into dollars it is restated using the retail price index. This produces a value of (50 million × 1000/100)/220 = $2,272,727.

This method adjusts the value of the complex to reflect the effect of 10-fold inflation over the 2-year period. In this way the 'disappearing assets' problem is overcome. In fact, the asset now appears to be worth more than when it was first acquired.

Solution 7.3: Ant

Evaluation of issues (a)–(c)

(a)   Tax losses

The tax loss is governed by IAS 12 *Income Taxes*, and would be classified as a temporary difference as the transactions giving rise to the tax loss have already been included in the financial statements. These transactions will have future tax consequences, as tax relief will be available if the subsidiary eventually makes taxable profits. A flow of benefits could potentially flow to the group so, under IAS 12, the potential deferred tax implications could be recorded as a deferred tax asset.

Under IAS 12, more care or prudence must be considered before recording a deferred tax asset. A recoverability test needs to be applied first. It must be more likely than not that there will be suitable taxable profits which can absorb the deductible temporary difference. There is little indication that demand for the company's product will be reversed in the foreseeable future, thus no asset should be created at this stage and the $6m should therefore be reversed. The journal entry is recorded below. If circumstances were to change favourably in the future, then it might eventually be recorded again on the balance sheet. In any case, it should not have been offset against deferred tax liabilities from other jurisdictions unless there is a legal right of set-off.

Dr	Taxation (income statement)	$6m	
Cr	Deferred taxation (non-current liabilities)		$6m

(b) *Foreign exchange transactions*

Under IAS 21 *The Effect of Changes in Foreign Exchange Rates*, the loan from the German bank is classified as a monetary liability which must be retranslated at the rates of exchange ruling at the balance sheet date. The loan would have to be restated from its original carrying value of 25$m (40m Francos/1.6) to $26.67m (40m Francos/1.5), resulting in an exchange loss of $1.67m to be reported in the income statement and included within financing.

The net assets in the investment country must be translated using the rate of exchange at the year end (closing rate) as the subsidiary is relatively independent of the parent. At the year end the net assets are the same as on the date of investment, as the investment has remained at 40m Francos. Once translated at $1.5 the assets are recorded at $26.67m and an exchange gain of $1.67m recorded. This must be taken direct to equity under IAS 21.

Where a foreign currency loan is used to finance a foreign currency equity investment then IAS 39 requires hedge accounting to be adopted, and exchange differences are recorded in reserves until such time as the subsidiary is disposed. At that time the differences are recycled through the income statement as part of the overall gain/loss on disposal. There are, however, very stringent rules that must be adhered to regarding the setting up of the hedge and measuring its effectiveness throughout its life.

The correcting journal entry should be as follows:

Dr	Investments in subsidiary	$1.67m	
Cr	Long-term loans		$1.67m

(c) *Issue of loan notes*

The issue of two million $100 loan notes is a compound financial instrument, and IAS 32 *Financial Instruments: Disclosure and Presentation* requires such instruments to be classified in two component parts in the balance sheet of the issuer. That requirement is regardless of whether or not the issuee is likely to exercise his or her option. The fair value of the option to convert should be valued first ($22.5m in this case), and deducted from the total outstanding to find out the value of the debt.

Under IAS 39 *Financial Instruments: Recognition and Measurement*, financial liabilities that are held for trading should be initially measured at cost but are then fair valued with any gains/losses being recorded in the income statement. The initial cost represents the proceeds received less any issue costs – i.e. $175.5m (2m notes × $100 × 90% issue price = $180m − $4.5m issue costs). The loan element is the difference between the value of the option of $22.5m and the total cost initially recorded of $175.5m, giving rise to a loan of $153m. Since the loan is held to maturity, the accounting treatment is to remeasure the liability at amortised cost using the effective interest method to measure the annual finance cost. The finance cost should be a constant percentage of the outstanding loan for each period.

Working

Initial amount of loan	$153m
Terminal loan repayment (2m × $135 per note)	270m
Annuity factor $153/$270m	0.567
Annuity tables – effective annual rate for 5 years	12%
Finance cost in year 1 12% × $153m	$18.36m
Closing loan outstanding at the end of Year 1 ($153 + 18.36)	$171.36m

Journal entries

			$m	$m
1.	Dr	Capital and reserves	4.5	
	Cr	Income statement		4.5

Being the reversal of incorrect write off of issue costs to the income statement

			$m	$m
2.	Dr	Loan notes	180	
	Cr	Capital and reserves		180

Being the reversal of previous incorrect entry of loan notes entirely credited to long-term liabilities

			$m	$m
3.	Dr	Capital and reserve	175.5	
	Cr	Loan		153
		Capital reserves		22.5

Being correct split between option element and loan element of the convertible loan notes

			$m	$m
4.	Dr	Finance costs (income statement)	18.36	
	Cr	Loan		18.36

Being the first year's finance charge based on the effective rate of interest of 12%

8

Taxation – solutions

Solution 8.1: H

(a) Notes *re* current taxation and deferred tax for year ended 30 April 2002

Tax on profit on continuing operations – income statement note

	$ million	$ million
Current tax		
Income tax on profits for the year		0.40
Deferred tax		
Reversal of temporary differences	(0.08)	
Effect of a change in tax rate	(0.05)	
		(0.13)
Total tax charge		0.27

Deferred tax – balance sheet note

	$ million
Provision as at 30 April 2001	0.69
Deferred tax credit in income statement for the year	(0.13)
Provision as at 30 April 2002	0.56

Working

  Deferred tax

	$ million
Temporary differences as at 30 April 2001	2.30
Temporary timing differences as at 30 April 2002	2.00
Deferred tax as at 30 April 2001 (2.30 × 30%)	0.69
Deferred tax as at 30 April 2002 (based on new rate of 28% × 2.30)	0.64
Reduction in deferred tax provision	0.05
Temporary difference for 2002 (2.30 − 2.00 = 0.30 × 28%)	0.08

(b) Why might a deferred tax asset be recognised on the balance sheet for the company pension scheme?

Pension costs represent a temporary timing difference for deferred tax purposes. The creation of a provision for pension costs is not payable for many years but is still recognised as a cost of employment in the financial statements that is charged in the income statement. However, the company does not get tax relief on the pension schemes until they are actually paid, which may not be for many years to come.

There is therefore a current charge against income, but its associated tax relief is deferred until future years. This creates a timing difference, as the company will pay less tax in the future when the payment is made for the pension costs. There is therefore a potential deferred tax asset in this situation.

(c) Why is a reconciliation of actual tax paid to potential tax payable a useful note to the financial statements?

If one were to examine the accounting profit for the year and apply the current potential tax that would be due on those profits, it would be assumed that this should add up to the current tax payable to the government. However, companies do not pay tax on accounting profits. They pay tax on taxable profits, which are calculated by the Inland Revenue on a different basis than the accounting profits. Companies will have to add back depreciation to their accounting profits and then claim whatever capital allowances are permitted by the Revenue. Similarly, they have incurred losses in the past which they are now using to reduce the current tax payable. There are a large number of items which result in a lack of symmetry between accounting and taxable profits.

The rationale for the tax reconciliation statement is to help users and investors understand the extent to which a company has been able to make use of the current tax regime to reduce their potentially high accounting profit to a substantially lower taxable profit, or *vice versa*, by utilising tax losses and excess capital allowances. There are also a number of permanent differences of which the reader should be aware – examples include disallowed expenditure for tax such as entertaining and certain legal expenses, and the exclusion from taxable profit of government grants. The reconciliation should make it clear what has caused the overall difference between accounting and taxable profits by splitting up the differences, particularly between permanent and timing differences.

Solution 8.2: Payit

(a) Why were the flow-through and partial provision methods rejected by the IASB?

There have been three different methods suggested as to how to account for deferred taxation:

1. The flow-through method
2. The partial provision method
3. The full provision method.

Flow-through method

Under the first method, the tax liability recognised in the financial statements is merely the current tax liability or charge for the period and no provision is made for deferred tax. It is obviously very simple in that it rejects the notion of deferred tax, but it has a number of disadvantages:

1. It leads to wide fluctuations in the tax charge dependent largely on government fiscal policy.
2. It fails to recognise that government policy merely postpones the payment of tax. It is not free of tax and thus understates the liabilities owed.
3. It fails to match the tax incurred during the period to the income earned – i.e. the matching or accruals principle.

Partial provision method

This method was adopted by the ASB in SSAP 15, and it merely requires a provision for deferred tax to be created when timing differences reverse in the foreseeable future. If they can be rolled over, they do not need to be provided. It is a halfway house between flow-through and full provisioning. The IASB rejected this approach for the following reasons:

1. It fails to accord with Framework in that it understates the true amount of liabilities owed. If timing differences are rolled over, it is argued that these can be discounted back to present value instead. Unfortunately the IASB has rejected discounting on the basis of costs outweighing any benefits received.
2. The method depends largely on management expectations, in that they must forecast when timing differences are likely to reverse via budgets/forecasts and then provide for the tax at that time. It is very easily manipulated by management.

As a result, the IASB has plugged for full provision as the only acceptable method of accounting for deferred tax.

(b) The logic underlying the IAS 12 treatment of revaluations and fair value adjustments

IAS 12 takes a temporary timing difference approach to accounting for deferred tax. Effectively this means that deferred tax is recognised only when a timing difference emerges, even though it may never be paid. The revaluation of a fixed asset could lead to capital gains tax being paid, but only if the asset is sold and no rollover relief has been claimed. IAS 12, however, demands it be provided for; FRS 19 does not. FRS 19 takes a liability view, and argues that no legal or constructive obligation exists until the asset has been sold and no rollover relief claimed.

A similar problem arises in fair value adjustments. Fair value by itself does not create a liability. It would only be incurred where, on acquisition, the reporting entity entered into a binding agreement to sell the asset that was revalued on consolidation. However, IAS 12 demands that the potential tax be provided for, as it is a temporary timing difference.

(c)   The effect of particular transactions on the deferred tax amounts in the consolidated balance sheet of Payit

Transaction 1

The inter-company sale will give rise to a provision for unrealised profit on the unsold inventory on consolidation. The amount should be $10m \times 20\% \times 25\% = \$500,000$. This provision must be made in the consolidated accounts. However, this profit has already been taxed in the financial statements of Payit. A timing difference therefore emerges, and this will crystallise when the stock is sold outside the group in the following year. The provision will be reversed but no tax will be incurred. The timing difference therefore gives rise to a deferred tax asset of $30\% \times \$500,000 = \$150,000$.

Deferred tax assets are only recognised to the extent that they can be recovered – the doctrine of prudence. An asset can only be created on the basis that it is more likely than not that suitable taxable profits will exist from which the reversal of the timing difference can be deducted.

Transaction 2

Unrelieved tax losses give rise to a timing difference as the loss is recognised in the financial statements but tax relief will follow in the future if the company generates sufficient taxable profits to offset the losses.

The amount of the deferred tax asset to be carried forward is therefore $25\% \times \$8m = \$2m$.

Similarly to Transaction 1, however, there must be sufficient probability of future profits before an asset is recognised.

Solution 8.3: Cohort

Deferred tax implications of given information for the Cohort Group of companies

General

When a reporting entity acquires other companies, the deferred tax charge must be reviewed in relation to the enlarged group as a whole. For example, individual companies may not be able to recognise a deferred tax asset for taxable losses but they may be able to avail of group relief if the acquiree brings in taxable profits. A provision, therefore, should be made for all differences between the fair values of Air's assets acquired ($4m) and their tax base ($3.5m). However, no provision will be required on the temporary difference arising on the recognition of non-tax deductible goodwill of $1 (\$5m − \$4m).

Cohort is planning to list on the Stock Exchange, but with no new shares issued. It will be subject to tax rates for public companies (at 35%), and thus the liability must be based on the tax rates that are expected to apply when the liability is settled or the asset realised. The tax rates, however, must be substantially enacted by parliament.

Acquisition of Air

(i) *Database*

It seems unlikely that this intangible asset of $0.5m will be allowed for tax, even though the directors will claim tax relief for it. There is a possibility that the company will have to return the excess allowance claimed, and thus a liability should be recognised.

(ii) *Intra-group profit on goods sold*

Included in inventory is inter-company profit of $0.6m ($1m profit × $1.8m/$3m). This is eliminated from inventory resulting in a difference between the book value $1.2m and its tax base of $1.8m, thus $0.6m × current tax rate should be provided.

(iii) *Unremitted profits of subsidiaries*

Under IAS 12 *Income Taxes*, tax must be provided on unremitted earnings if the parent company is unable to control the timing of the remittances or if it is probable that remittance will take place in the foreseeable future. Cohort, however, controls the payment of dividends and it would not normally recognise the deferred tax liability. However, as the profits are to be distributed, and tax would be payable on the amount remitted, then a provision for deferred tax should be made.

Acquisition of Legion

(i) *Gains/losses on readily marketable government securities*

When a portfolio of investments is revalued in excess of its previous carrying value, a temporary difference will emerge if the tax on the surplus differs from the accounting treatment. The gain has been recorded within income but it is not taxed until realised, thus a temporary difference emerges. That difference of $4m gives rise to a deferred tax liability and the related expense is charged against revenue, not equity.

(ii) *General bad debt provision on loan portfolio*

A temporary difference emerges as the accounting expense will not be allowed for tax. As the provision is likely to increase in the future, the timing difference will not reverse in the short term. However, a deferred tax asset of $2m × current tax rate should be provided, but it is still probable that taxable profits will be available against which the temporary difference can be utilised.

(iii) *Unused tax losses*

Unrelieved tax losses can create a deferred tax asset. Deferred tax assets should be recognised to the extent that they can be regarded as recoverable. Recoverability is based on all the evidence available and to the extent that it is probable that the deferred tax asset will be realised. If it is probable that either all or only part of the deferred tax asset will be realised, then a deferred tax asset should be recognised for that amount. Future realisation depends on the existence of future sufficient taxable profits. It will need to be reduced by any amount that is considered probable to be realised.

Solution 8.4: DT

(a) Explain what the terms 'balance sheet focus' and 'temporary differences' mean in relation to deferred taxation

IAS 12 *Income Taxes* has adopted a 'balance sheet approach' to accounting for deferred tax in line with the Framework of the IASB. It is based on the principle that a deferred tax liability or asset should be recognised if the recovery of the deferred tax asset or payment of the deferred tax liability will result in higher or lower tax payments in the future. Deferred tax should be calculated as the difference between the tax base and its current book value.

Differences between the book value of the asset/liability and its tax base are called 'temporary differences'. The term 'temporary' is used because an entity will realise its assets and settle its liabilities over time, at which point the tax consequences will crystallise.

The objective of the temporary difference approach is to recognise the full future tax consequences of temporary differences on the balance sheet.

(b) Discuss the arguments for and against discounting long-term deferred tax balances

Deferred tax involves a temporary postponement of the tax liability, and it is possible, therefore, to regard the deferred tax liability as equivalent to an interest-free loan from government to be repaid at some time in the future. This temporary benefit or loan should be reflected by discounting the liability and recording a lower tax charge so as to take into account the time value of money. This is the treatment adopted for most other liabilities. The discount would then be amortised over the period of deferment. The purpose of discounting is to measure future cash flows at their present value, and therefore deferred tax balances can only be discounted if they can be viewed as future cash flows that are not already measured at their present value.

Some short-term temporary differences clearly represent future tax flows (e.g. accruals paid in the following period) and do not need to be discounted, and others are already discounted (e.g. retirement benefits).

However, the major temporary difference is whether or not to discount deferred tax in the case of accelerated tax depreciation. It is argued that this temporary difference does not give rise to a future cash flow, and thus there is no basis for discounting. Alternatively, one view is that accelerated tax depreciation is a liability that will be repaid in the form of higher tax assessments for the future.

Discounting, however, makes the deferred tax computation more difficult to calculate and more subjective. There are enormous additional costs in scheduling and calculating deferred taxation as well as in determining an appropriate discount rate. IAS 12, therefore, specifically prohibits discounting on the grounds of cost/benefit considerations.

(c) Calculation of the deferred tax liability

	Book value	Tax base	Temporary differences
	$m	$m	$m
Property, plant and equipment (per ii)	2,600	1,920	680
Other temporary differences (per ii)			90
Subsidiary (per i)	76	60	16
Inventory (per i)	24	30	(6)
Property sold (165 × 1/0.3 gross) (per vi)			550
Liability for healthcare products	100	–	(100)
Unrelieved losses (per note iv)			(100)
Temporary differences			1,130
Deferred tax liability 1,320 × 30% (680 + 90 + 550)			396
16 × 25%			4
asset (200) × 30% (100 + 100)			(60)
(6) × 25%			(1.5)
			338.5

Tax charge for the charge

Opening deferred tax liability	280
Closing balance 338.5 less tax on goodwill	434.5
Charge for the year	54.5

Notes:
The unrelieved tax losses of $34m + 56m = 100 × 1/0.3 gross = $300m will be available for offset against the current year's profits ($110m) and against the 2002 accounts of $100m. Due to the uncertainty *re* available taxable profits in 2002, no deferred tax asset can be recognised for any losses which may be offset against this amount. Thus a deferred tax asset may be recognised for the losses to be offset against taxable profits in 2001 – i.e. $100m × 30% = $30m.

Unrealised group profits eliminated on consolidation are provided at the receiving company's rate of tax of 25%.

The deferred tax provision will rise in total by $335.5m ($338.5m − $3m), which reduces net assets, distributable profits and post-tax earnings. The profit for the period will be reduced by $54.5m, which would probably be substantially more under IAS 12 than the previous method. A prior year adjustment of $280 − 3m is required, as IASs are being applied for the first time (**IFRS** 1). The impact of the increased borrowing on balance sheet may well affect gearing considerably, and thus there is a need to look into existing loan covenant agreements and perhaps at increasing the equity of the business of cutting dividends or increasing the capital base.

9

Group accounting – solutions

Solution 9.1: Rod, Reel and Line

(a) IAS 19 Employee Benefits

	$m
Current service cost	110
Interest cost on scheme liabilities	20
Expected return on scheme assets	(10)
Overall charge to income statement	120

		$m
Scheme assets		
Cash contributions		100
Expected return on assets		10
Actuarial gain (bal. fig.)		15
		125
Scheme liabilities		
Current service costs	110	
Interest costs	20	
		130
Deficit		(5)

IAS 19 requires a portion of the unrecognised gains and losses at the end of the previous reporting period to be recognised either using the 10% corridor approach or another systematic method including immediate recognition. The company does not have to recognise the actuarial gains as there were no operating gains, but in view of the significance of the extra charge for the pension scheme in the income statement, immediate recognition is the best policy. However, in that case, it must be credited outside the income statement and instead in equity.

The shareholders funds should be reduced by $105m ($120 − 15m) and the double entry is recorded as below:

Dr		Reserves	105m	
	Cr	Trade receivables		100m
		Pension liability		5m

(b) Consolidated balance sheet of Rod Plc as at 30 November 2002

	$m	$m
Non-current assets		
Tangible assets $(1,230 + 505 + 256 - 56 - 5)$		1,930
Intangible assets $(72 + 60 = 132 -$ amortised 84) $(W1)$		48
		1,978
Current assets		
Inventory $(300 + 135 + 65 - 20$ development)	480	
Trade receivables $(240 + 105 + 49 - 100$ pension contrib.)	294	
Cash in hand and at bank $(90 + 50 + 80)$	220	
		994
Total assets		2,972
Capital and reserves		
Called up share capital		1,500
Share premium		300
Accumulated profits $(W2)$		502
Minority interest $(155 + 109.6)$ $(W2)$		265
		2,567
Non-current liabilities $(135 + 25 + 20)$		180
Current liabilities $(100 + 70 + 50)$		220
Pension liability		5
Total equity and liabilities		2,972

Working

W1 Shareholdings

			Rod		
				80%	1/12/1999
1/12/2000		40%	Reel		
				25%	
			Line		
Direct minority in Reel		20%			
Direct minority in Line		35% + indirect minority 20% × 25%			

W2 Acquisitions
Acquisition of Line (60%):

	$m		$m
Cost of investment – direct	160	Share capital (60%)	120
Cost of investment – indirect		Share premium (60%)	30
(80% × 100)	80	Accumulated profits	
		(50 × 60%)	30
		Goodwill	60
	240		240

Goodwill 60/4 years = 15 per annum × 2 years = 30 amortised.

Minority interest (40% Line):

	$m		$m
Cost of investment		Share capital (40%)	80
(20% × 100)	20	Share premium (40%)	20
		Accumulated profits	
		(60 × 40%)	24
		Excess depreciation	
Consolidated B/S	109.6	(14 × 40%)	5.6
	129.6		129.6

Acquisition of Reel (80%):

	$m		$m
Cost of investment – direct	640	Share capital (80%)	400
		Share premium (80%)	80
		Accumulated profits	
		(100 × 80%)	80
		Fair value adjustment	
		(710 − 700 × 80%)	8
		Goodwill	72
	640		640

Goodwill 72/4 years = 18 per annum × 3 years = 54 amortised.

Minority interest – Reel (20%)

	$m		$m
Development w/off		Share capital (20%)	100
(20 × 20%)	4	Share premium (20%)	20
Trade discount	1	Accumulated profits	
Consolidated B/S	155	(200 × 20%)	40
	160		160

Accumulated profits:

		$m		$m
Minority interests:	– Reel	40	Balance – Rod	625
	– Line	24	Balance – Reel	200
Cost of control:	– Reel	80	Balance – Line	60
	– Line	30	Excess depreciation (14 × 60%)	8.4
Development costs w/off				
(20 × 80%)		16		
Trade discount (6 − 1depr. × 80%)		4		
Fair value adjustment				
(10 × 80%)		8		
Pension scheme		105		
Goodwill w/off (30 + 54)		84		
Consolidated B/S		502.4		
		893.4		893.4

W3   Calculation of revaluation reserve eliminated
Line:

	Revaluation	**Cost**
Cost	300	300
Depreciation – 2001	(50) (1/6th)	(50)
NBV 30.11.2001	250	250
Revaluation surplus	70	
NBV post-revaluation	320	
Depreciation – 2002	64 (20%)	50 (original cost)
NBV 30.11.2002	256	200

The revaluation reserve of 70 is eliminated and reserves increased by excess depreciation of $64 - 50 = 14$, leaving a net reduction in value of tangible non-current assets of 56.

Solution 9.2: Hydrox

(a)   Consolidated balance sheet of Hydrox as at 31 March 2000

	$000	$000
Assets		
Non-current assets		
Property, plant and equipment (*W1*)		45,840
Goodwill (1,200/6 years = 200 × 2 = 400 amortised = 800 net)		800
Investments (1,000 + 6,000 + (90% × 8,000 − 6,000))		8,800
		55,440
Current assets		
Inventory (9,500 + 4,000 + goods in transit 600 × 100/120)	14,000	
Trade accounts receivable (7,200 + 1,500 − 2,000 *W2*)	6,700	
Cash and bank (300 + nil)	300	
		21,000
Total assets		76,440
Equity and liabilities		
Share capital and reserves		
Equity shares of $1 each		10,000
Reserves		
Accumulated profits (*W3*)		34,510
		44,510
Minority interest (W4)		1,130
Non-current liabilities		
12% Debentures	4,000	
Bank loan	6,000	
		10,000

Current liabilities

Trade accounts payables (6,700 + 5,200 − 1,400) (W2)	10,500	
Bank overdraft	4,500	
Provision for income tax (4,100 + 700)	4,800	
Provision for dividends	1,000	
		20,800
Total equity and liabilities		76,440

NB: Proposed dividends in the future, under IAS 10, will not be permitted to be recorded on the balance sheet nor in the income statement, as they are only contingent and not full liabilities. Instead they should be noted in the financial statements.

Working

W1 Property, plant and equipment ($'000)

Balance – Hydrox	26,400	Additional depreciation	
Balance – Syntax	16,200	($5.4m/5 years × 2)	2,160
Fair value (90% × $6m)	5,400	Consolidated B/S	45,840
	48,000		48,000

W2 Current accounts ($'000)

Trade payables	1,400	Trade receivables	2,000
Goods in transit	500		
Accumulated profits			
(unrealised on stock)	100		
	2,000		2,000

W3 Accumulated profits ($'000)

Unrealised profit	100	Balance – Hydrox	48,600
(20/120 × 600)		Balance – Syntax	6,300
Additional deprec.(*W1*)	2,160		
Cost of control			
(90% × 4,000 dividend)	3,600		
Minority interest			
(10% × 6,300)	630		
Cost of control			
(90% × 15,000)	13,500		
Goodwill amortised ((1,200/6 years) × 2)	400		
Consolidated B/S	34,510		
	54,900		54,900

NB: There are no post-acquisition profits from which to pay a dividend, so the dividend of £4,000 must have been paid out of pre-acquisition profits.

W4 Minority interest ($'000)

		Equity shares (10%)	500
Consolidated B/S	1,130	Acc. profits (10%)	630
	1,130		1,130

W5 Cost of control ($'000)

Investments in Syntax	30,000	Equity shares (90%)	4,500
		Acc. profits (90%)	3,600
		Acc. Profits	13,500
		Fair value adjustments	
		(90% × $6m + $2m)	7,200
		Goodwill	1,200
	30,000		30,000

(b) Specific matters raised by Brand and Company

Fall in stock market value of Syntax's investments

There appears to be a massive fall in the value of Syntax's investments. These investments may well recover, but the size of the fall is dramatic and it would be unlikely that the stock market recovery will be to their former level. They should be written down to their recoverable amount.

Bank loan

The bank loan is crystallising and thus should be treated as an actual rather than contingent liability.

Deterioration of operating performance in Syntax

The going concern of Syntax is clearly in doubt, and this has several implications for the group:

- the carrying value of the investment in Syntax should be written off; this will also affect consolidated goodwill;
- if Syntax were to go into receivership, then the guarantee given by Hydrox is likely to crystallise;
- the dividend declared by Syntax could be considered illegal, as it is deliberately prejudicial to the company's creditors.

Solution 9.3: Hanford

(a) Consolidated balance sheet as at 30 September 2001

	$000	$000
Non-current assets		
Goodwill (6,250 − 625) (*W1*)		5,625
Property, plant and equipment (78,540 + 27,180 + 3,000 FV − 360 (*W2*))		108,360
		113,985
Current assets		
Inventory (7,450 + 4,310)	11,760	
Accounts receivable (12,960 + 4,330 − 820 inter-co.)	16,470	
Insurance claim (*W1*)	600	
Cash and bank (nil + 520)	520	
		29,350
Total assets		143,335

Equity and liabilities
Capital and reserves

Ordinary shares of $1 each (20,000 + 5/3 × 8,000 × 75%)	30,000
Reserves	
Share premium (10,000 + (25m acq. − cash 5m − capital 10m))	20,000
Accumulated profits (*W3*)	65,575
	115,575
Minority interest (W4)	5,950

Non-current assets

8% Loan note 2004 (nil + 6,000)	6,000

Current liabilities

Trade accounts payable (5,920 + 4,160 − 620 inter-co.)	9,460	
Bank overdraft (1,700 + nil)	1,700	
Dividend payable to minority (800 × 25%)	200	
Provision for taxation (1,870 + 1,380)	3,250	
*Proposed final dividend	1,200	
		15,810
Total equity and liabilities		143,335

*This should now be treated as a contingent liability, not as a full liability.

Working

W1   Cost of control (75%)

Investment in Stopple	25,000	Ordinary shares	6,000
		Pre-acquisition dividend (*W3*)	150
(Cash 5,000 + 5/3 × 6m		Share premium	1,500
= 2m × $10)		Pre-acq. profits	
		(6,000 + 1/2 × 8,000) × 75%	7,500
		Fair value adjustments	
		($4m + 0.8m × 75%)	3,600
		Goodwill	6,250
	25,000		25,000

The fair value adjustment requires that only Hanford's share of the excess value of the land be recognised as a fair value adjustment – i.e. 75% × $4m = $3m. Although the insurance claim is a contingent asset, IAS 22 requires Hanford to assess all assets and liabilities at the date of acquisition. The best estimate of the claim is full settlement of $800,000. However, the benchmark treatment requires that only Hanford's share of this be included in the consolidated financial statements, i.e. $600,000.

Goodwill of $6.25m must be amortised over 5 years, but on a time apportionment basis – i.e. 1/2 year ($6.25m/5 years = $1.25m × 1/2 = $625,000).

W2 Unrealised profit on sale of plant

Hanford sold an asset for $2.4m but it cost $2m. The unrealised profit of $0.4m would have been depreciated by 10% since it was acquired, thus $40,000 was over-depreciated. The net effect is an adjustment of $360,000.

W3 Accumulated profits

Unrealised profit – plant	360	Balance – Hanford	63,260
Administration costs	200	Balance – Stopple	14,000
Minority interest (25% × 14,000 – 200)	3,450	Dividend from Stopple	*450
Cost of control			
(6,000 + 8,000 × 1/2) × 75%	7,500		
Goodwill amortised(*W1*)	625		
Consolidated B/S	65,575		
	77,710		77,710

*Stopple's dividends for the year are $1,200,000 (400,000 + 800,000). The post-acquisition element is $450,000 ($1.2m × 75% × 6/12). The pre-acquisition element of the final dividend is $800,000 × 75% = 600,000 − 450,000 = 150,000.

W4 Minority interest (25%)

Consolidated B/S	5,950	Ordinary shares – Stopple	2,000
		Share premium – Stopple	500
		Accumulated profits – Stopple	3,450
	5,950		5,950

W5 Inter-company accounts

Accumulated profits		Trade accounts receivable	820
(administration expenses)	200		
Trade accounts payable	620		
	820		820

(b) Reasons why a parent company may wish not to consolidate a subsidiary company

The reasons why a parent may not wish to consolidate a subsidiary can be broken down into two broad categories:

1. To improve the reported position of the group i.e. gearing
2. To comply with IAS 27 *Consolidated Financial Statements and Separate Financial Statements*.

Improvement of financial position

The financial position could show operating losses, poor liquidity position or high gearing. If the subsidiary were to be consolidated it would proportionately worsen the group position, thus tempting the parent to avoid consolidation.

IAS 27

Subsidiaries should legitimately be excluded from consolidation, but only for the following reasons:

1. The subsidiary operates under severe long-term restrictions. It does not have control over the subsidiary's ability to transfer funds to the parent – e.g. nationalisation, exchange control restrictions.

2. Control is intended to be temporary because the investment is held exclusively with a view to its subsequent resale.

The former reason is obviously not permitted by IASs, whereas the latter is.

IAS 27 also makes specific reference to subsidiaries sometimes being excluded on the basis of differing activities. Companies that have adopted this approach tend to argue that to add such subsidiaries together could lead to a misleading impression. IAS 27 does not permit exclusion on these grounds because it feels that 'differing activity' problems are overcome by the provision of segmental information.

Solution 9.4: Hydrate

(a)   Acquisition accounting

Consolidated income statement for the year ended 30 September 2002

		$000
Sales revenue	(24,000 + 6/12 × 20,000)	34,000
Cost of sales	(16,600 + 6/12 × 11,800)	(22,500)
Gross profit		11,500
Operating expenses	(1,600 + 6/12 × 1,000 + 3,000 goodwill amortisation)	(5,100)
		6,400
Taxation	(2,000 + 6/12 × 3,000)	(3,500)
Profit for the year		2,900

Consolidated balance sheet as at 30 September 2002

		$000	$000
Non-current assets			
Property, plant and equipment	(64,000 + 35,000)		99,000
Investments	(nil + 12,800 + 5,000 fair value adjustment)		17,800
Goodwill (*W1*)	(30,000 − (30,000/5 years = 6,000 × 1/2 year))		27,000
			143,800
Current assets			
Inventories	(22,800 + 23,600)	46,400	
Trade accounts receivables	(16,400 + 24,200)	40,600	
Cash and bank	(500 + 200)	700	
			87,700
Total assets			231,500
Equity and liabilities			
Ordinary shares of $1 each	(20,000 + 12,000 × 5/4)		35,000
Reserves			
Share premium	(4,000 + 12,000 × 5/4 × $5)	79,000	
Accumulated profits	(57,200 + 4,200 × 6/12 − 3,000 gw)	56,300	135,300
			170,300
Non-current liabilities			
8% Loan notes	(5,000 + 18,000)		23,000
Current liabilities			
Trade accounts payable	(15,300 + 17,700)	33,000	
Taxation	(2,200 + 3,000)	5,200	38,200
			231,500

Working

W1   *Cost of control*

	$000		**$000**
Investment in Sulphate		Ordinary shares	12,000
(12m × 5/4 = 15m × $6)	90,000	Share premium	2,400
		Accumulated profits	
		(42,700 − 2,100 post-acq.)	40,600
		Revaluation reserve	
		(fair value adjustment)	5,000
		Goodwill	30,000
	90,000		90,000

Amortisation of goodwill $30,000/5 years = $6,000 per annum × 1/2 year = $3,000.

(b)   Uniting of interests (merger) accounting

Consolidated income statement for the year ended 30 September 2002

		$000
		44,000
Sales revenue	(24,000 + 20,000)	44,000
Cost of sales	(16,600 + 11,800)	(28,400)
Gross profit		15,600
Operating expenses	(1,600 + 1,000)	(2,600)
		13,000
Taxation	(2,000 + 3,000)	(5,000)
Profit for the year		8,000

Consolidated balance sheet as at 30 September 2002

		$000	**$000**
Non-current assets			
Property, plant and equipment	(64,000 + 35,000)		99,000
Investments	(nil + 12,800)		12,800
			111,800
Current assets			
Inventories	(22,800 + 23,600)	46,400	
Trade accounts receivables	(16,400 + 24,200)	40,600	
Cash and bank	(500 + 200)	700	
			87,700
Total assets			199,500
Equity and liabilities			
Ordinary shares of $1 each	(20,000 + 12,000 × 5/4)		35,000
Reserves			
Share premium	(4,000 + 2,400)	6,400	
Accumulated profits	(57,200 + 42,700 − 3,000 adj.,		
	shares issued 15,000 − 12,000)	96,900	103,300
			138,300
Non-current liabilities			
8% Loan notes	(5,000 + 18,000)		23,000

Current liabilities

Trade accounts payable	(15,300 + 17,700)	33,000	
Taxation	(2,200 + 3,000)	5,200	38,200
			199,500

(c) Description of distinguishing features of a uniting of interests and whether the combination should be treated as a merger or not

The distinguishing features of a uniting of interests are as follows:

1. It is not possible to identify an acquirer. Instead the shareholders of the combining enti-ties unite in a substantially equal arrangement to share control over the combined entity.
2. All parties to the combination participate in the management of the combined business.
3. The sizes of the combining parties should be broadly the same, leading to a substan-tially equal exchange of voting common shares. This is to ensure that no one party is in a position to dominate the combined business due to its previous relative size.
4. There must not be a significant reduction in the rights attaching to the shares of one of the combining parties, as this would weaken the position of that party.

The above is generally evidenced by the following:

*   the substantial majority of voting shares are exchanged or pooled;
*   the fair value of one entity is not significantly different from that of the other parties;
*   the shareholders of each party maintain substantially the same voting rights relative to each other in the new combined entity;
*   no party's share of the equity of the combining entities should depend on the perfor-mance of their previous business;
*   all parties should share in the future prosperity of the business.

In this particular situation the following observations can be made in deciding whether or not a uniting of interests could be acceptable:

*   the use of the phrase 'compatible partner companies' could be an indicator of a uniting of interests;
*   the sizes of the companies are broadly the same (20,000 to 15,000 shares);
*   the consideration is all in the form of equity shares and satisfies the share exchange criterion;
*   the composition of the new management team and whether or not rank is shared equally would need to be determined from the details and terms of the combination agreement.

Solution 9.5: Humbug

(a) Consolidated balance sheet as at 30 September 2001

	$000	**$000**
Non-current assets		
Property, plant and equipment	(11,250 + 4,800 + (1,800 × 6/12)	
	+ (80% × 700 less 2/5ths × 700) − 15)	17,271
	unrealised profit)	

Software	(80% × 300 less 160, i.e.80% × 200)		80
Goodwill (*W1*)	1,000 − 400 + (500 − 100)		1,000
			18,351
Investments	(6,000 + 400 − 4,250 Spyder − 1,500 Juke Box)		650
			19,001
Current assets			
Inventories	(1,120 + 640 + 50% × 600)	2,060	
Trade accounts receivable	(950 + 380 + 50% × 320)	1,490	
Cash and bank	(180 + 50% × 280)	320	
			3,870
Total assets			22,871
Equity and liabilities			
Ordinary shares of $1 each			5,000
Reserves			
Accumulated profits (*W2*)			13,311
			18,311
Minority interests (W3)			880
Non-current liabilities			
10% Loan notes	(50% × 500)		250
Current liabilities			
Trade accounts payable	(1,300 + 850 + 50% × 400)	2,350	
Taxation	(560 + 350 + 50% × 100)	960	
Bank overdraft		120	3,430
Total equity and liabilities			22,871

Working

W1   Cost of control (80% Spyder)

	$000		$000
Investment in Spyder (2,000 × 80% × $2.50)	4,000	Ordinary shares	1,600
Investment in loan notes (500 × 50%)	250	Loan notes (50%)	250
		Accumulated profits	600
		(750 × 80%)	
		Fair value adjustments	
		(700 × 80%)	560
		(300 × 80%)	240
		Goodwill	1,000
	4,250		4,250

Goodwill is amortised over a 5-year period, resulting in a charge of $200,000 per annum for 2 years = $400,000.

W2   Accumulated profits

	$000		$000
Unrealised profit (equipment)		Balance – Humbug	12,640
(200 × 25/125 × 50% × 3/4 years)	15	Balance – Spyder	2,400
Depreciation – equipment		Share of joint venture	
(700 × 80% × 2/5 years)	224	(500 × 50%)	250

Depreciation – software		
(300 × 80% × 2/3 years)	160	
Minority interest (20% × 2,400)	480	
Cost of control (80% × 750)	600	
Goodwill amortisation (*W1*)	400	
Goodwill amortisation		
(joint venture – see below)	100	
Consolidated B/S	13,311	
	15,290	15,290

The joint venture – Juke Box

Investment in Juke Box	(1,000 ordinary shares × 50% × $3)	$1,500
Net assets at acquisition	(1,000 shares + 1,000 accumulated profits × 50%)	
		1,000
Goodwill on acquisition		500

Amortisation 500/5 years = 100 per annum.

The benchmark treatment in IAS 31 requires proportional consolidation to be adopted for joint ventures, and the benchmark treatment in IAS 22 requires that only the group share of 80% of the fair value adjustments be included in non-current assets.

W3   Minority interest (20%)

	$000		$000
		Ordinary shares	400
		Accumulated profits	
Consolidated B/S	880	(20% × 2,400)	480
	880		880

(b)   Explain, with illustrations, the relevant features and accounting treatment of jointly controlled operations and jointly controlled assets in IAS 31

Jointly controlled operations

Under such joint ventures each venturer contributes its own assets, incurs its own expenses and raises its own finance. The contractual arrangement usually contains rules for the sharing of the revenues from the operations of the venturers. The joint venture is not a separate legal entity. An example is the European consortium of Airbus Industries, whereby five European companies each manufacture different parts of the aircraft and share the revenues from their sale. The accounting treatment of such joint ventures is that each separate venturer recognises the assets and liabilities they contribute and the income and expenses they earn and incur. The treatment is the same in both the entity and in the consolidated accounts.

Jointly controlled assets

This involves the joint control of an asset or a related group of assets. The assets will provide benefits to the joint venturers, in the form of either a service or revenues earned. The joint venture is not a separate entity. A typical example is an oil pipeline where several companies contribute to its construction and operation in return for the right to transport their own oil through the pipeline. Another example may be the joint ownership and operation of an investment property where each joint venturer takes a share of the rental income. The accounting treatment is for a joint venturer to recognise its share of any jointly controlled assets classified according to the nature of the asset, not as an investment in a joint venture. An oil pipeline would be incorporated in property, plant and equipment. Similar principles would apply to the recognition of liabilities, incomes and expenses relating to the joint venture and to both the entity's and the consolidated financial statements.

Solution 9.6: Holding

(a) Consolidated balance sheet of Holding as at 31 March 2002

		$000	$000
Non-current assets			
Property, plant and equipment	(12,000 + 12,200 + 5,400 − 300 + 4,000 − 1,000)		32,300
Goodwill (*W1*)	(1,800 − 300)		1,500
			33,800
Current assets			
Inventories	(11,250 − (3,000 × 20/120 × 1/2))	11,000	
Trade accounts receivables	(3,600 + 2,300 − 700)	5,200	
Cash and bank		150	
			16,350
Total assets			50,150
Equity and liabilities			
Ordinary shares of 25 cents each			5,000
Reserves			
Accumulated profits (*W2*)			25,850
			30,850
Minority interests (W3)			2,400
Non-current liabilities			
12% Loan notes	(nil + 6,000 + 600 − 200 interest)		6,400
Current liabilities			
Trade accounts payable	(6,250 + 3,700 − 700)	9,250	
Bank overdraft	(nil + 1,250)	1,250	10,500
Total equity and liabilities			50,150

Working

W1   Cost of control (75%)

	$000		$000
Investment in Sandham	8,850	Ordinary shares	1,500
Revaluation – loan		Cost of control (75% × 4,000)	3,000
(600 × 75%)	450	Revaluation – plant (75% × 4,000)	3,000
		Goodwill	1,800
	9,300		9,300

Goodwill of $1,800 is depreciated over 6 years = $300 per annum.

W2 Accumulated profits

	$000		$000
Depreciation – inv. prop.			
(5,400/18 years)	300	Balance – Holding	27,150
Revaluation surplus		Balance – Sandham	5,000
(6000 – 5,400)	600	Interest adjustment	200
Depreciation – plant			
(4,000/4 years)	1000		
Unrealised profit – invent.			
(3,000 × 20/120 × 1/2)	250		
Minority interest			
(25% × 5,000 + 200 – 1,000)	1,050		
Cost of control (75% × 4,000)	3,000		
Goodwill amortised	300		
Consolidated B/S	25,850		
	32,350		32,350

W3 Minority interest (25%)

	$000		$000
Revaluation – loan (25% × 600)	150	Ordinary shares	500
Consolidated B/S	2,400	Revaluation – plant	
		(25% × 4,000)	1,000
		Accumulated profits	1,050
	2,550		2,550

Property, plant and equipment is made up as follows:

Balance – Holding	12,000
Balance – Sandham	12,200
Investment property (see below)	5,400
Depreciation of property (5,400/18 years)	(300)
Revaluation of plant	4,000
Depreciation (25% × 4,000 1 year)	(1,000)
	32,300

Under IAS 40 *Investment Properties*, once a property is let to a group member it ceases to be classified as an owner-occupied property and is therefore no longer an investment property. It should be transferred at carrying value of $5.4m and then depreciated over its remaining life of 18 years. The revaluation surplus of $600,000 for this year ($6m − $5.4m) must be removed from accumulated profits, as prior to this, under the fair value model, surpluses would have been included in income.

(b) Brand recognition

(i) Whether a brand should be included in Sandham's financial statements

The recognition of brands in an entity's financial statements is governed by IAS 38 *Intangible Assets*. That standard states that intangible assets can only be recognised where they embody future economic benefits that will flow to the entity and the cost of the assets can be measured reliably. Also, internally generated brands should not be recognised as assets. Thus Sandham should not recognise its brand despite its value being supported by independent consultants.

(ii)   Whether a brand should be recognised in the consolidated financial statements of Holding and its subsidiaries at 31 March 2002

As regards the consolidated accounts, this is governed by **IFRS 3** *Business Combinations*, which requires all of a subsidiary's identifiable assets and liabilities to be recognised at fair value on the consolidated balance sheet at the date of acquisition. IFRS 3 permits fair values to be determined by an active market or 'on a basis that reflects an amount that the enterprise would have paid for the asset in an arm's length transaction'. IAS 38 specifically says that certain enterprises have developed techniques for valuing brands and similar assets, and these techniques can form the basis of a fair valuation of a brand on acquisition.

The board of Holding was not aware of the brand (or at least its value) at the date of acquisition, and thus did not include it in its consolidated balance sheet. However, IFRS 3 does permit assets and liabilities that were not recognised at the time of acquisition to be subsequently recognised where additional evidence becomes available. This may occur up to the end of the first full accounting period commencing after the acquisition. Applying this logic it means that it may be possible for Holding to recognise the brand in the consolidated financial statements to 31 March 2002.

A further problem, however, also arises. IFRS 3 limits the amount that may be recognised as an intangible asset, whose value is determined other than by reference to an active market, to a value that does not create negative goodwill. In this case it means that although there is a valuation of $3m for the brand, Holding can only recognise $1.8m (i.e. equal to the amount of goodwill on acquisition). Any amount above that figure would create negative goodwill, and this is not permitted.

By recognising the brand on the balance sheet, this effectively would replace goodwill. The consequences of this are that the brand would be depreciated over 30 years, whereas goodwill was depreciated over 6 years. IAS 38 further requires that where the estimated life of an intangible asset is greater than 20 years, the entity must conduct an annual impairment review of that asset.

Solution 9.7: Hyper

(a)   Calculation of consolidated goodwill – acquisition of Syphon and Andean

Goodwill in Syphon

	$m	$m
Investment at cost (80% × 30 shares × $8.70)		208.8
Less pre-acquisition dividend (80% × 10 × 9/15)		(4.8)
Fair value of net assets acquired		204
Ordinary share capital	30	
Pre acquisition reserves (40 + 100 × 9/15)	100	

Revaluation reserve – land (20 + 5)	$\frac{25}{155} \times 80\%$	(124)
Goodwill		80

Goodwill should be amortised for the year ended 30 September 2002 equal to $80m/5 years × 6/12ths = $8m.

Goodwill in Andean

	$m	$m
Investment at cost (40% × 20 shares × $6)		48
Fair value of net assets acquired		
Ordinary share capital	20	
Pre acquisition reserves (14 + 36 × 6/12)	32	
Revaluation reserve – plant	$\frac{18}{70} \times 40\%$	(28)
Goodwill		20

Goodwill should be amortised for the year ended 30 September 2002 equal to $20m/5 years × 6/12ths = $2m.

(b) Consolidated income statement for Hyper for the year ended 30 September 2002

	$m
Sales revenue (420 + (375 × 6/15) − 20 inter-co.)	550.0
Cost of sales 320 + (190 × 6/15) − 20 inter-co. + (20 × 25/125 × 50% = 2 profit)	378.0
Gross profit	172.0
Operating expenses (40 + (30 × 6/15) + 8 goodwill amortised)	(60.0)
Interest (12 + (10 × 6/15))	(16.0)
Associated company	
(40% × 48 × 6/12 = 9.6 − (18 / 3 yrs × 40% × 6/12 = 1.2) − 2 goodwill)	6.4
Profit before tax	102.4
Income tax 20 + (35 × 6/15) + (12 × 40% × 6/12)	(36.4)
Profit after tax	66.0
Minority interests (110 × 20% × 6/15)	(8.8)
Net profit for the period	57.2

IAS 28 *Accounting for Investments in Associates* requires income from associates to be disclosed on the face of the income statement, but it does not specify where it should be positioned or whether it should be pre- or post-taxation. The above includes the associate's income as a gross of tax figure before the income tax charge, and the group's share of the associate's tax has been included in the income tax charge.

(c) Calculation of the carrying value of the investment in Andean

	$m
Investment at cost	48.0
Post-acquisition profit before tax	6.4
Less share of income tax (12 × 6/12 × 40%)	(2.4)
	52.0

This is represented by net assets at 30 September 2002 of 70 + fair value adjustment net of depreciation of $18m − ($18m/3 years × 6/12) = $15m = $85m × 40% = $34m + goodwill unamortised of $20m − 2m amortised = $52m.

Solution 9.8: Pulp, Fiction and Truth

(a) Consolidated income statement for the year ended 31 December 2000

	Pulp	Fiction	Truth Subsidiary (3/12)	Associate (9/12)	Adjustments	Total
	$000	**$000**	**$000**	**$000**	**$000**	**$000**
Revenue	30,000	32,000	7,000		(500) (*W1*)	68,500
Cost of sales	(15,000)	(16,000)	(3,500)			(34,500)
Gross profit	15,000	16,000	3,500			34,000
Other operating						
Expenses	(8,000)	(8,500)	(1,500)		400 (*W1, W2*)	(17,600)
Profit from						
Operations	7,000	7,500	2,000		(100)	16,400
Share of profit						
of associate						
(40% × 8,000 × 9/12)				2,400	(40) G'w	2,360
(40/75 × 75) (*W2*)						
Investment income	2,850				(2,600) (*W3*)	250
Interest payable	(1,000)	(1,200)	(250)	(300) 40%		(2,750)
Profit on disposal	4,400				(2,678) (*W4*)	1,722
Profit before tax	13,250	6,300	1,750	2,100	(5,418)	17,982
Income tax expense						
(1,900 + *500)	(2,400)	(1,900)	(500)	(600) 40%		(5,400)
Profit after tax	10,850	4,400	1,250	1,500	(5,418)	12,582
Minority interest						
(25% × 1,250)			(312)			(312)
Group profit	10,850	4,400	938	1,500	(5,418)	12,270

*Tax on disposal.

(b) Consolidated statement of changes in equity for the year ended 31 December 2000

	Pulp	Fiction	Truth Subsidiary (3/12)	Associate (9/12)	Adjustments	Total
	$000	**$000**	**$000**	**$000**	**$000**	**$000**
Opening equity	24,500	5,900	5,250		(1,950) (*W5*)	33,700
Group profit	10,850	4,400	938	1,500	(5,418)	12,270
Dividends	(3,000)	(2,000)		(600) 40%	2,600	(3,000)
Adjustment			(6,188)	3,300	2,888 (*W4*)	–
Closing equity	32,350	8,300	–	4,200	(1,880)	42,970

Working

W1 Inter-group transactions: administration charge

Fiction (100 × 4)	400
Truth (to 31 March 2000)	100
	500

W2 Goodwill

	Fiction (100%)		Truth (75%)	
	$000	$000	$000	$000
Cost of investment		13,000		12,000
Issued capital	4,000		8,000	
Share premium	3,000		4,000	
Fair value adjustment	1,000		—	
Accumulated profits	3,000		2,000	
	11,000		14,000	
Group share (100%/75%)		(11,000)		(10,500)
		2,000		1,500

W3 Investment income

	$000	
Fiction (100%)	2,000	
Truth (40% × 1,500)	600	
Other (non-group)	250	bal. fig.
	2,850	

W4 Profit on disposal of truth

	$000	$000
Proceeds on sale		10,000
Net assets sold		
Issued capital	8,000	
Share premium	4,000	
Accumulated profits at 1 January 2000	9,000	
Profit for 3 months to 31 March 2000	1,250	
(3/12 × 5,000)	22,250	
Share of net assets sold (35%)		(7,788)
Unamortised goodwill (35/75 × (1,500 − 450 6 yrs))		(490)
		1,722

W5 Opening equity

	$000	$000
Pulp (15m capital + 9.5 reserves)		24,500
Fiction (100% × (15,900 − 10,000 pre-acq.))		5,900
Truth (75% × (21,000 − 14,000))		5,250
Less: fair value adjustment (Fiction)		(1,000)
		34,650

Less: goodwill – Fiction (2,000 / 20 yrs = 100 × 5 yrs)   500
       – Truth (1,500 × 40/75 = 800/20 yrs = 40 × 7 yrs)   450
                                                    (950)
                                             33,700

W6   Closing equity

	$000	$000
Pulp (24,500 + 3,950)	28,450	
Add: net gain on disposal (4,400 − 500 tax)	3,900	
		32,350
Fiction (100% × (18,300 − 10,000 pre-acq.))		8,300
Truth (40% × (24,500 − 14,000))		4,200
Less: fair value adjustment (Fiction)		(1,000)
		43,850
Less: goodwill – Fiction (2,000 / 20 yrs = 100 × 6 yrs)	600	
– Truth (1,500 × 40/75 = 800 / 20 yrs = 40 × 7 yrs)	280	
		(880)
		42,970

Solution 9.9: Harden

(a)   Consolidated balance sheet of Harden as at 30 September 2000

	$000	$000
Non-current assets		
Property, plant and equipment (*W1*)		6,440
Patents (250 + 420)	670	
Goodwill (180 − 72) (*W4*)	108	778
Investments		
Associated company (*W6*)	912	
Other investments (150 + 200)	350	1,262
		8,480
Current assets		
Inventories (*W2*)	962	
Trade receivables (420 + 380 − 70 − 50)	680	
Bank	150	1,792
Total assets		10,272
Capital and reserves		
Equity shares of $1 each	2,000	
Reserves		
Share premium	1,000	
Accumulated profits (*W3*)	5,052	8,052
Minority interest (20% × 3,400 − 50)		670
Non-current liabilities		
Deferred tax		200

Current liabilities

Trade payables (750 + 450 − 70) (*W5*)	1,130	
Taxation	140	
Bank overdraft	80	1,350
		10,272

Working

W1 Tangible fixed assets

	$000
Harden	3,980
Solder	2,300
Fair value adjustment – land (80% × 200)	160
	6,440

W2 Inventories

	$000
Harden	570
Solder	400
Less unrealised profit (140 × 40/140 × 1/2 × 40%)	(8)
	962

W3 Accumulated profits

	Harden $000	Solder $000		Harden $000	Solder $000
Unrealised profit (*W2*)	8		Balance	4,500	1,900
Management charge (*W5*)		50	Share of associate		
Minority interest			(*W6*)	160	
(20% × 1,900 − 50)		370			
Cost of control					
(80% × 1,200)		960			
Goodwill amortised					
Solder (*W4*)	72				
Active (*W7*)	48				
Consolidated B/S	4,532	520			
	4,660	1,900		4,660	1,900

W4 Cost of control (80% Solder)

	$000		$000
Investment at cost – Solder	2,500	Equity shares	800
		Share premium	400 (500 × 80%)
		Accumulated profits	960 (1200 × 80%)
		Fair value adjustments	160 (200 × 80%)
		Goodwill	180
	2,500		2,500

Goodwill is amortised over 5 years − $180,000/5 years = $36,000 for 2 years = $72,000.

W5   Current accounts – elimination of inter-company balances

	Dr	**Cr**
Trade payables	70	
Accumulated profits – Solder	50	
Trade receivables		120

W6   Associated company – goodwill and carrying value

	$000
Investment at cost	800
Net assets at acquisition (40% × 500 + 100 + 800)	(560)
Goodwill	240
Goodwill is amortised at 20% × 240 = 48 for 1 year	
Investment at cost	800
Share of post acquisition profit (40% × (1,200 − 800))	160
	960
Amortisation of goodwill	(48)
	912
Or share of net assets (1,800 × 40%)	720
Share of goodwill (240 − 48)	192
	912

(b)   Specific issues for directors to discuss on trading losses and insurance claims

IFRS 3 *Business Combinations* regulates that the assets and liabilities recognised on acquisition are only those that existed at the date of acquisition. That logic is applied to the two issues in items (i) and (ii):

(i) Trading losses available for future tax relief can represent a deferred tax asset, but only where their recovery can be assured with a high degree of certainty. Prior to acquisition there was a certain amount of uncertainty and the directors are correct in not recognising a deferred tax asset *re* the losses. However, when Deployed becomes a member of the Harden group, deferred tax must be assessed on a group basis and the directors of Harden are confident that the tax losses of Deployed are utilised on a group basis. IFRS 3 states that any benefit to the group of an acquired entity's tax losses should be recognised at acquisition. A deferred tax asset of $60,000 (i.e. $200,000 × 30%) should be recognised as part of the fair value exercise. This can be treated either as a reduction in the group deferred tax liability or as a deferred tax asset provided it meets the criteria in IAS 12 *Income Taxes*.

(ii) The disputed insurance claim is not 'probable' and thus, under IAS 37 *Provisions, Contingent Liabilities and Contingent Assets*, should not be recognised. However, IFRS 3 states that identifiable assets and liabilities of the acquired entity have to be recognised in the consolidated accounts even if they were not recognised or did not qualify for recognition in the acquired company's own accounts. A contingent asset may become a recognised asset and thus be recognised as part of the fair value exercise at the best estimate of its likely outcome.

Solution 9.10: Horsefield

(a)　Consolidated balance sheet of Horsefield as at 31 March 2002

	$000	$000
Non-current assets		
Property, plant and equipment (8,050 + 3,600)		11,650
Licence (180 − 60 2 years amortisation)		120
Goodwill (1,170 − 468 2 years amortisation)		702
		12,472
Investments		
Associated company　　　　　(W5)	705	
Other investments		
(4000 + 910 − 3,240 Sandfly − 630 Anthill + 120 fair values)	1,160	1,865
		14,337
Current assets		
Inventories (830 + 340)	1,170	
Trade receivables (520 + 290 − 40 cash in transit)	770	
Bank (240 + 40 cash in transit)	280	2,220
Total assets		16,557
Equity and liabilities		
Equity shares of $1 each	5,000	
Accumulated profits　　　　　(W3)	8,203	13,203
Minority interest　　　　　(W2)		364
Non-current liabilities		
10% Loan notes (500 + 240)		740
Current liabilities		
Trade payables (420 + 960)	1,380	
Dividend payable to minority　(W3)	10	
Taxation (220 + 250)	470	
Proposed dividend	200	
Bank overdraft	190	2,250
		16,557

NB: Proposed dividends should be contingent liabilities not recorded as actual liabilities on balance sheet as from 1st January 2005 (IAS 10).

Working

W1　Cost of control

Investment in Sandfly (1,200 × 90% × $3)	3,240	Ordinary shares (90% × 1,200)	1,080
		Accumulated profits (90% × 800)	720
		Fair value adjustments (W4)	270
		Goodwill	1,170
	3,240		3,240

Goodwill should be amortised over 5 years at $234,000 per annum for 2 years = $468,000.

W2   Minority interest

Consolidated B/S	364	Ordinary shares (10% × 1,200)	120
		Accumulated profits	214
		Fair value adjustments (*W4*)	30
	364		364

W3   Accumulated profits

Unrealised profit on inventories	3	Balance – Horsefield	7,300
(65 × 2/3rds × 30/130 × 30%)			
Depreciation – licence (180/6 × 2 yrs) (*W4*)	60	Balance – Sandfly	2,200
Minority interest (10% × 2,200 − 60)	214	Proposed dividend	90
Cost of control (90% × 800)	720	Share of profit of associate	
Goodwill amortised – Sandfly (*W1*)	468	(600 × 1/2 × 30%)	90
Goodwill amortised – Anthill (*W5*)	12		
Consolidated B/S	8,203		
	9,680		9,680

Unrealised profit on inventory sold to the associate is $65,000 × 30/130 × 2/3 × 30% × = × $3,000.

The proposed dividend of Sandfly must be allocated as 10% ($10,000) to the minority and shown as a creditor, as it will be paid in the near future, and 90% ($90,000) should be credited to group reserves.

W4   Fair value adjustments

Cost of control (90% × 300)	270	Investment property	120
Minority interests (10% × 300)	30	Licence	180
	300		300

W5   Associated company (30% Anthill)

Investment at cost (600 × 30% × $3.5)	630	Share capital	180
		Accumulated profits	
		(800 + 600 × 1/2× 30%)	330
		Goodwill	120
	630		630

Amortisation of goodwill should be 120/5 years = 24 × 1/2 = 12

The carrying value of the investment in the associate should be:

Share of net assets in associate	(30% × 2,000 − 3 unrealised profit)	597
Share of unamortised goodwill	(120 − 12)	108
		705

(b) The matters to be considered in determining whether an investment in another company constitutes associated company status

For an investment to be classified as an associate company, an entity must have 'significant influence' over the investee. Significant influence is presumed to exist where there is a holding of 20% or more of the voting power unless the investor can clearly demonstrate that this is not the case. Conversely, a holding of less than 20% is presumed not to be an associate unless it can be demonstrated clearly that the investor can exercise significant influence. Voting rights can be held directly or indirectly or through subsidiaries. IAS 28 *Accounting for Investments in Associates* excludes subsidiaries and joint ventures from the definition of an associate. These are covered by other separate accounting standards. The 20% test is not conclusive evidence of significant influence, and other factors must also be considered. These include decisions as to whether the investing company:

- has representation on the board of the investee;
- participates in the policy-making decisions of the investee;
- has material transactions with investees; or
- provides managerial personnel or technical expertise to the investee.

Solution 9.11: Portal

(a) Consolidated income statement for Portal Group for the year ended 31 May 2001

	$m	$m
Revenue (2000 + 1600 + 625 − 100 inter-co.)		4,125
Cost of sales (1500 + 1400 + 590 − 100 inter-co.		
− 2 stock profit − 15 goodwill − 2 depr.)		(3,409)
Gross profit		716
Distribution costs (120 + 40 + 13)	173	
Administrative expenses (100 + 36 + 17)	153	
		(326)
Profit from operations		390
Profit on disposal of shares in subsidiaries (*W7*)		15
Share of operating loss of associate (*W4*) (*W5*)		(11)
Interest expense (10 + 4 + 10)		(24)
Investment income (50 − 60% × 40)		26
		396
Income tax expense (90 + 36 + 3 + 40% × 3)		(130)
Minority interest (*W6*)		(25)
Net profit for the year		241

(b)   Group accumulated reserves at 31 May 2001

	$m
Portal reserves at 1 June 2000	350
Profit for the year	241
Dividends for the year	(20)
Hub reserves at 1 June 2000 (250 − 200 pre-acq. − 2 depr. − 4 inter-co. pft) × 75%	33
Goodwill written off	(10)
	594

Working

W1   Inter-group profit

The inter-company profit included in the opening inventory of Portal was $20 × 20% = \$4$m and the closing inventory was $30 × 20% = \$6$m. The \$2m excess is charged to cost of sales.

W2   Tangible non-current assets – Hub

Fair value increase (per note iii)		10
Additional depreciation 20% to reserves	2	
20% to income	2	4
		6

W3   Calculation of goodwill

		Hub	**Network**
Cost of investment		565	410
Net assets at acquisition (75% × 700)		(525)	
(80% × 450)			(360)
Goodwill		40	50
Amortised – Year 1 (25%)	10		
– Year 2 (25% × 1/2)	5		
– Year 2 (25% × 1/2 × 60/75)	4	(19)	(6) (50/4 × 120/140)
		21	
Written off on sale of shares (40 − 15 × 15/75)		(5)	(25) (50 × 120/240)
Closing balance		16	19

Goodwill amortised during the year is 5 + 4 + 6 = 15.

W4   Associated company – Network
Half year (1.12.2000 to 31.5.2001):

	$m
Operating profit for 1/2th year before taxation	5
Profit (40%)	2
Less interest payable (20 × 40% × 1/2 year)	(4)
	(2)
Tax on profit (6 × 40% × 1/2 year)	(1.2)
Loss for the period	(3.2)

W5   Impairment

	$m
Cost of investment in Network ($410m × 1/2)	205
Share of loss for year (16 × 40%)	(6.4)
Goodwill written off	(6)
	192.6
Value in use ($460m × 40%)	184
Impairment loss	(8.6)
Total impairment loss (8.6) + 2 profit − 4 interest	11

W6   Minority interest

	$m	$m
Hub – profit after tax	84	
– inter-group profit on inventory (6 − 4)	(2)	
– depreciation	(2)	
	80	
(1.6.2000 to 30.11.2000) 40 × 25%		10
(1.12.2000 to 31.5.2001) 40 × 40%		16
Network – loss $16m × 1/2 × 20%		(1.6)
		24.4

W7   Profit/loss on sale of investment

		Hub		**Network**	
	$	$	$	$	
Sales proceeds		140		200	
Cost of investment (15/75 × 565)		(113)		(205)	410 × 1/2 profit on
		27		(5)	disposal
Less opening reserves	250		100		
profit for half year	42		(8)		
profit on acquisition	(200)		(100)		
	92	(15%) (13.8)	(8)	3.2 (40%)	
Add goodwill written off					
(40 × 15/75 − 5)		3			
Depreciation (*W8*)		0.45			
		16.65		(1.8)	

Total profit is 16.65 − 1.8 = $14.85m.

W8   Additional depreciation on sale of shares

Depreciation – due to fair value increase as at 1.12.2000	$3
Reduction in reserves (3 × 15%)	$0.45

Solution 9.12: Vitalise

(a) Financial statements for Vitalise

Income statement of Vitalise for the year ended 30 September 2001

	$000
Sales revenue (3900 − 250) (*W1*)	3,650
Cost of sales (2500 − 100) (*W1*)	(2,400)
Gross profit	1,250
Operating costs (250 + 300) (*W2*)	(550)
Loss on investment property (*W5*)	(40)
Foreign exchange losses (*W4*)	(250)
	410
Finance costs (65 + 25 loan not sale + 13 conv. loan − *W1* and *W6*)	(103)
Profit before tax	307
Income tax (260 − 90 extra. item) (*W3*)	(170)
Profit for the period	137

Balance sheet of Vitalise as at 30 September 2001

	$000	$000
Non-current assets		
Property, plant and equipment (3810 − 250 *W4* − 35 *W5*)		3,525
Investment property (390 − 40)		350
		3,875
Current assets (1200 + 100) (*W1*)		1,300
		5,175
Equity and liabilities		
Share capital, capital and reserves:		
Ordinary shares $1 each		1,000
Option to convert (*W6*)		60
		1,060
Reserves		
Revaluation reserve (110 − 35)	75	
Accumulated profits	1,512	1,587
		2,647
Non-current liabilities		
8% Convertible loan note (440 + 13) (*W6*)	453	
Loan from Easyfinance (250 + 25 accrued int.) (*W1*)	275	728
Current liabilities		1,800
		5,175

Statement of changes in equity for the year ended 30 September 2001

	Share capital	Revaluation reserve	Accumulated profits	Total
	$000	$000	$000	$000
Balance at 1 October 2000	1,000	250	1,500	2,750
Share conversion option	60 (500 − 440)			60

Revaluation of investment Property transferred to realised profits (*W5*)		(140)	140	
Revaluation loss (410 − 375)		(35)		(35)
Profit for the period			137	137
Dividends			(265)	(265)
Balance at 30 September 2001	1,060	75	1,512	2,647

Working

W1   Sale to Easyfinance

There is no international standard on substance over form, but the Framework requires financial statements to reflect substance. The sale to Easyfinance is not a 'true' sale – it is a secured loan carrying interest at 10% per annum. The sale must be reversed, with goods going back into inventory and the proceeds treated as a loan as well as accruing interest of $25,000 for the current year.

W2   Extraordinary item

Under IAS 8 *Accounting Policies, Changes in Accounting Estimates and Errors*, no extraordinary items may now be recorded in financial statements. The abortive takeover expenses relating to Dunsters would therefore be recorded within normal operating activities. They may need to be disclosed in the notes, if material.

W3   Taxation

As the takeover costs are not extraordinary, its tax effects should be part of the tax charge on ordinary activities.

W4   Foreign currency

Vitalise has adopted the closing rate of exchange to translate the value of the aircraft and its related creditor. This is incorrect, as IAS 21 *The Effects of Changes in Foreign Exchange Rates* requires that assets are translated at historic acquisition rates $500,000 (FrF3m/6) not $750,000 (FrF3m/4), leading to a foreign exchange loss of $250,000 to be reported in the income statement. IAS 21 and SIC 11 do permit the loss to be included as part of the cost of the asset, but only where there is a severe devaluation and there is no practical means of hedging or settling the liability. This is not likely in the case of Vitalise.

W5   Properties

The fair value model in IAS 40 *Investment Property* requires that the movement in invest-ment properties be reported in the income statement (i.e. loss of $40,000). This differs from IAS 16 *Property, Plant and Equipment*. which requires surpluses/deficits to be recorded as movements in a revaluation reserve. IAS 40 also requires reclassification of any investment property revaluation reserve surplus (i.e. $140,000 ($390,000 − $250,000)).

W6   Convertible loan

Under IAS 32 *Financial Instruments: Disclosure and Presentation*, a convertible loan is treated as a compound instrument with elements of both equity and debt. It must be reflected as such in the financial statements. The debt should be valued via discounted cash flow analysis with any residue allocated to equity.

	Cash flows	Factor (12%)	Present value
Year 1 interest	40	0.88	35.2
Year 2 interest	40	0.78	31.2
Year 3 interest	40	0.70	28.0
Year 4 interest, redemption	540	0.64	345.6
Total value of debt component			440.0
Proceeds of the issue			500.0
Equity component (residual amount)			60.0

For the year ended 30 September 2001, the interest cost in the income statement should be increased from $40,000 to $53,000 (12% of $440,000) by accruing $13,000, which should be added to the carrying amount of the debt.

(b)   Calculation of Earnings Per Share

Basic EPS

Earnings

Profit after tax = $137,000

Number of shares:
Although the bonus issue occurs after the year end, IAS 33 *Earnings Per Share* requires that it should be included in the calculation of the EPS. The denominator would therefore be 1.2m (1,000 × 6/5).

Earnings per share

($137,000 × 100)/1.2 = 11.4c

Diluted EPS

Earnings

As per basic	$137,000
Add loan interest saved ($53,000 (*W6*)) − ($40,000 × 30% tax relief)	41,000
	178,000

Number of shares

As per basic	1.2m
Shares under conversion option	0.5m
	1.7m

Earnings per share

($178,000 × 100)/1.7m = 10.5c

Solution 9.13: Inventure

(a) The nature and acceptability of the accounting practices set out in (i) to (iv)

(i) *Pooling of interests versus acquisition accounting*

IAS 22 *Business Combinations* originally governed the rules in deciding whether or not a business combination should be accounted for as a 'pooling of interests' or as an 'acquisition'. Where an acquirer could not be identified, then a uniting of interests could have been indicated. SIC9 made it clear that all relevant facts and circumstances surrounding the transaction had to be considered. Single characteristics such as relative size and voting power of the combining enterprise could not be viewed in isolation, or be individually determinate.

Essentially there had to be a continual mutual sharing in risks and benefits, which meant, for example, sharing in the management of the combined enterprise. In this case, the press portrayed the share-for-share exchanges as an acquisition, although this may not have been at the instigation of either management team. The relative sizes of the combining enterprises could not be so disparate that one party dominated the combined entity by virtue of its relative size. The market capitalisation of the two companies is in the ratio 65 : 32 and the fair value of the net assets in the ratio 60 : 30. Therefore, one would presume that Inventure was the dominant party (this presumption was retractable if sufficient evidence was available).

All parties to the transaction had to participate in the management structure for the combined entity. The new management team have all been drawn from Inventure. However, as the board was made up entirely of personnel from Inventure, this would seem to indicate an acquisition even though the board was agreed by both parties.

The share exchange transaction did not satisfy the conditions of IAS 22 in terms of pooling of interests, as the price paid ($35m) was above the market value of Melia's shares ($32m) and there was not substantially an equal exchange of voting ordinary shares. Taking into account the fact that the combination was portrayed as an acquisition, that the sizes of the parties are quite disparate and that the management of the new undertaking comprises the directors of Inventure, then it seems as though this was not a pooling of interests but an acquisition.

	$m
Market price of Inventure's shares – 10m × $3.50	35
Fair value of net assets	(30)
Goodwill	5
Amortisation of goodwill per annum	$1.25m

(ii) *Reorganisation costs*

The company has treated the purchase and resale of Caster as a group reorganisation, and has ignored the requirements of IAS 31 *Financial Reporting of Interests in Joint Ventures* and IFRS 3 *Business Combinations*. Caster had been purchased from a non-group company on 1 June 2001. Subsequently, Caster was sold to a group company for a loss. This loss is an inter-group loss and should be eliminated from the income statement. The joint venture should be accounted for under IFRS 3/IAS28/31, which requires fair values to be attributed to the investeee's underlying assets and liabilities, and thus goodwill recognised. Pooling of interests would not be permitted, especially as Melia itself could not adopt that technique.

In the income statement, joint ventures should report the results of the joint ventures using the 'equity' method under IAS 31. Unlike pooling, only half of the results for the period will be included in the pre-tax earnings in the income statement. Thus profit after taxation will effectively fall by $300,000 plus the amortisation of goodwill, and there will be a corresponding reduction in minority interest. The adoption of the equity method will effect the calculation of key ratios such as EBITDA, as only half of the profit and tax expense will be included rather than the full results.

The amortisation of goodwill will be as follows:

	$m
Purchase consideration	30
Net assets at fair value ($58m/2)	29
Goodwill	1
Amortisation over 4 years	$0.25m

Total amortised is $250,000 + $1.25m = $1.5m.

(iii) *Operating lease*

IAS 17 *Leases* requires operating lease rentals to be charged to the income statement on a straight-line basis over the lease term, irrespective of when the payments are made. A large upfront payment by the lessee should be allocated to the period over which the benefit is earned. The prepayment should be included in current and not non-current assets. It should not be included in depreciation at a figure of $40,000 ($200,000/5 years), but should be included in the rental expense at this figure. Comparability will be affected if the classification of the premium results in high amortisation and low rental expense, particularly if EBITDA is adopted as a performance measure.

(iv) *Retirement benefit scheme*

No provision for the fine should be made, as the entity does not have either a legal or a constructive obligation to pay the fine. It can be avoided by simply setting up a retirement benefit scheme. If it is not in place by next year, a provision, however, would have to be set up to pay the fine. By providing now, it would be accounting for a future loss.

Both IAS 19 *Employee Benefits* and the actuaries recommend using high-quality corporate bond rates to discount the future retirement benefit liability. As the bond rates are currently low, this produces a high liability. As the scheme is funded by a mix of equity and bonds, this will produce a better return than bonds alone; however, the retirement fund may have a market value less than the liability. Thus it may be advisable to consider moving to a defined contribution scheme where the entity's only commitment is the annual contribution and the entity is not committed to account for any shortfalls in employee pensions. The risk is effectively passed on to the employee.

(b) Impact on current earnings of changes recommended in (a)(i)

Revised income statement for the year ended 31 May 2002

	$000
Revenue (5,740 − 1,500 joint venture)	4,240
Cost of sales (3,215 − 700 joint venture)	(2,515)
Gross profit	1,725
Distribution and administration expenses	
(675 + 1,500 amortisation − 100 joint venture)	(2,075)
Loss from operations	(350)
Share of operating profit of joint venture (50% × 700)	350
Interest payable	(60)
Profit on disposal of non-current asset investments	70
Profit before tax	10
Income tax expense (225 − 100 JV + 100 × 50% JV)	(175)
Loss after tax	(165)
Minority interests (550 − 50% × 600 joint venture)	(250)
Net loss for the period	(415)

NB: Amortisation 1,250 Melia and 250 Caster = 1,500.

(c) The adoption of EBITDA as a performance measure

EBITDA (earnings before interest, tax, depreciation and amortisation of goodwill) is now widespread as a measure of performance. The use of EBITDA restricts the advantage of adopting pooling of interests, as the increase in depreciation caused by fair value reporting and the amortisation of goodwill are removed from the ratio. EBITDA is also used by analysts, as non-cash items are removed.

In this case, the company has attempted to enhance earnings by the following:

- using pooling of interests to avoid goodwill;
- the treatment of exceptional reorganisation costs and the avoidance of a retirement benefit cost;
- the capitalisation of the $200,000 initial payment on the operating lease increases depreciation but minimises operating costs.

Solution 9.14: Bloomsbury

Bloomsbury income statement for the year to 30 September 2002

	$000	$000
Sales revenue (98,880 − 7,200) (*W1*) + 800 (*W2*)		92,480
Cost of sales (*W1*)		(61,700)
Gross profit		30,780

Other operating income:		
Agency commission (*W1*)		720
Investment income – surplus on investment property (*W3*)	500	
Investment income – other	700	1,200
Operating expenses	(14,000)	
Loss on revaluation of property (*W3*)	(2,000)	
Loan interest (1,800 + 1,800 accrued)	(3,600)	
Preference dividends (500 + 500 accrued (*W5*))	(1,000)	
		(20,600)
Operating profit		12,100
Taxation (5,000 − 600 deferred tax (*W4*))		(4,400)
Net profit for the period		7,700

Bloomsbury – statement of changes in equity for the year ended 30 September 2002

	Share capital	Revaluation reserve	Investment property reserve	Accumulated profits	Total
	$000	**$000**	**$000**	**$000**	**$000**
Balance at 1 October 2001	40,000	nil	2,000	6,100	48,100
Surplus on revaluation of property (*W3*)		12,000			12,000
Net profit for the period				7,700	7,700
Ordinary dividends (*W5*)				(5,800)	(5,800)
Transfer to realised profits (*W3*)		(600)	(2,000)	2,600	nil
Balance at 30 September 2002	40,000	11,400	nil	10,600	62,000

Bloomsbury – balance sheet as at 30 September 2002

	$000	$000
Non-current assets		
Property, plant and equipment (*W3*)		90,800
Investments – investment property (10,000 + 500)		10,500
		101,300
Current assets		
Inventory	7,500	
Accounts receivable (16,700 − 1,200 + 120 (*W1*) + 200 (*W2*))	15,820	
Cash	500	23,820
Total assets		125,120
Equity and liabilities		
Ordinary shares of 25c each		40,000
Reserves:		
Accumulated profits	10,600	
Revaluation reserve (12,000 − 600) (*W3*)	11,400	22,000
		62,000
Non-current liabilities (*W7*)		41,500

Current liabilities

Trade and other payables (*W6*)	11,820	
Taxation	5,000	
Proposed dividends (*W5*)	4,800	21,620
Total equity and liabilities		125,120

Working

W1   Cost of sales

As per trial balance	56,000
Less adjustment for agent sales	(5,400)
Depreciation – leasehold (see *W3*)	4,400
Depreciation – plant and equipment (see *W3*)	6,300
Share of joint venture cost of sales	400
	61,700

The Brandenberg contract is a sales commission contract, and thus total sales of $7.2m and cost of sales of $5.4m must be removed from sales and cost of sales respectively. Similarly, accounts receivable of $1.2m must also be removed. In its place commission of 10% × $7.2m = $720,000 should be recorded in income and the balancing figure of $120,000 treated as accounts receivable due.

W2   Joint venture with Waterfront
Under IAS 31 *Financial Reporting of Interests in Joint Ventures*, the joint venture should be accounted for as a jointly controlled operation. As such, each party should account for its own share of assets, liabilities and results according to the terms of the agreement – i.e. proportionately consolidated.

W3   Non-current assets
Leasehold property:
Where a company chooses to revalue a non-current asset, it must revalue all the assets of the same class. In this case, therefore, Bloomsbury must recognise the fall in the value of the 15-year leasehold factory.

25-year lease – surplus	$12m	($52m − (50m − 10m))
15-year lease – deficit	$(2m)	($18m − (30m − 10m))

The revaluation deficit must be charged to income; it cannot be offset against the surplus on the other asset. A transfer, however, from revaluation reserve to retained profits must be made on the other asset as it is realised ($12m/20 years remaining life = $600,000) per annum.
     The properties will now be recorded on balance sheet as follows:

	Revalued amount	**Depreciation**	**NBV**
25-year lease	$52m	$2.6m (20 yrs)	$49.4m
15-year lease	$18m	$1.8m (10 yrs)	$16.2m
	$70m	$4.4m	$65.6m

Investment property:
Under IAS 40 *Investment Properties*, movements in the fair value of investment properties must be taken to income. Also, any previous surplus must be transferred to realised profits.

Plant and equipment:

	$000
As per trial balance	49,800
Share of joint venture	1,500
	51,300
Accumulated depreciation 1.10.2001	(19,800)
	31,500
Depreciation for the year (20% × 31,500)	(6,300)
Net book value at 30.9.2002	25,200

W4   Deferred taxation

The temporary timing differences have fallen by $2m, causing a reversal of deferred tax of $2m × 30% = $600,000. This reduces the tax charge for the year and the deferred tax liability from $2.1m to $1.5m.

W5   Dividends

Preference dividends (10% × $10m × 6/12)	500
Interim ordinary (bal. fig.)	1,000
Final proposed:	
– preference	500
– ordinary (40m × 4 × 3c)	4,800
	6,800

W6   Current liabilities

Accounts payable as per trial balance	9,420
Share of joint venture creditors	100
Accrued loan interest (10% × $18m)	1,800
Accrued preference dividend	500
	11,820

W7   Non-current liabilities

12% Loan note	30,000
10% Redeemable preference shares (*W4*)	10,000
Deferred tax (2,100 − 600) (*W4*)	1,500
	41,500

10
Disclosure standards – solutions

Solution 10.1: Portico

(a) The objectives and usefulness of reporting segment information

The objective of IAS 14 *Segment Reporting* is to enable users of financial statements to obtain a better understanding of past performance by enabling users to better assess the entity's risks and returns as they relate to the individual segments of the business. Segment information enables a more informed judgement about the enterprise as a whole.

Consolidated data 'hide' information about how each of the major parts of the business is performing. There is a need to disaggregate the consolidated data to see which segments are profit making, and which are subject to significantly different levels of liquidity, gearing etc.

In addition, over the last 30 years there has been a growth of multinational companies, and users need to find out how different geographical regions are performing.

Diversified operations represent distinct products or markets with distinct risks and returns, and it would be impossible to assess the effect these individual segments have had on past performance and their likely effect on future performance without having the information disaggregated.

(b) Definition of a reportable segment

A business segment is a distinguishable component of an enterprise which provides an individual product or service that is subject to different risks and returns from other business segments. In deciding how to split segments, consideration should be given to the nature of the product, the production processes, the type of customer, the distribution methods and the regulatory framework.

A geographical segment is a distinguishable component of an enterprise which provides products or services within a particular geographical environment that is subject to risks and rewards that are different from other geographical segments. Factors include economic, political, exchange control and foreign currency risks etc. These segments can be based on location of operations (by source) and on location of markets (by destination).

A reportable segment should contribute 10% or more of the enterprise's figures for:

- sales revenues;
- results (profits or losses);
- total assets.

If the aggregate of segments satisfying the 10% thresholds is less than 75% of the total enterprise, then smaller segments become reportable segments until the 75% level is reached or exceeded.

(c)   Main problems of providing segment information

The definition of a reportable segment: although defined in the standard, it is the responsibility of the directors to decide what the reportable segments should be and on what basis they should be reported. This obviously leads to considerable subjectivity and possible lack of comparison with other companies.

Cost allocation and apportionment: decisions about how and which costs to apportion are subjective, but there must be a 'reasonable basis' on which to allocate costs. If it is too difficult, the costs should not be apportioned but instead treated as unallocated and deducted from total segment results.

Interest costs: segment results should normally exclude interest charges. However, where the interest forms a fundamental part of a segment's results it should be included within the segment's results.

The definition of net assets: interest-bearing assets and liabilities should not be allocated, nor should common assets if they cannot be directly apportionable to segments.

(d)   Identification of reportable segments

There are three segments in excess of the 10% threshold:

Engineering	23%
Textiles	22%
Chemicals	20%
	65%

This is still under the 75% threshold, so there is a need to include both the travel Agency segment (8%) and house building (7%).

Recommendation on how the following items should be dealt with

(i) *Utility costs*: these should be allocated to the individual segments, as there is sufficient evidence on which to make an accurate allocation of costs (i.e. via invoices).

(ii) *Research and development costs*: this is clearly a central overhead, and any apportionment is purely arbitrary. There is no obvious connection between research and development and turnover. They should not be allocated.

(iii) *Leasing*: the leased assets can be specifically allocated to separate segments and would appear to be allocable. However, it can be argued that leasing is an integral part of the total overall financing and therefore should not be allocated.

Solution 10.2: Global

Report for the Chief Executive Officer of Global

To: Chief Executive Officer, Global
From: Management Accountant
Date: 31 July 2004
Subject: Segmental analysis

Introduction

With reference to your memorandum of the 20 July 2004, I am attaching my analysis of the performance of the main segments of the group as presented in IAS 14 *Segment Reporting*. Each of the segments are investigated in turn.

European segment

The profitability has declined from 10.1% to 9.7%, but this not particularly material. The return on capital employed has also declined marginally from 21.6% to 20%. However, in order to find out why this has occurred an analysis of detailed costs would be required and this not required by IAS 14. It could be due to higher wages costs, exchange rate differences or even higher interest costs. It is the segment with the highest turnover, and it has risen slightly over the last year.

There is no difference in asset turnover or in liquidity ratios from previous years, and, in comparison with American and African segments, liquidity is slightly worse but asset turnover is better.

American segment

The profitability of this segment has also slightly deteriorated over the year, from 16.1% to 14.8%, and ROCE from 27.3% to 25%. The margins are slightly higher than in Europe, but this may reflect lower wages costs. One significant change has been the doubling of profit in the associates in the segment, but there is no indication of the causes thereof.

The asset turnover has remained steady at 1.70 times per annum, and similarly liquidity shows virtually the same acid test ratio of 2.4 per annum. Again there is no detailed analysis of the figures, and further breakdowns would be required to be undertaken to analyse performance properly.

African segment

This segment is clearly the section of the business that needs to be controlled better. Analysis reveals current losses, albeit those losses have been halved in percentage terms (from 22% to 10%), and this is reflected in a doubling of turnover – thus spreading the fixed costs over a greater number of sales. However, it is still in deficit, and further improvement is vital to its ultimate survival.

The segment's liquidity is actually quite strong – in fact, more could be made of its current assets and greater control over stocks and debtors could help reduce the costs of obsolescence and bad debts.

One important feature is its high dependence on the other segments. No less than 10% of its sales come from the other segments, so any decision to discontinue the segment should be considered very carefully if it would have a material detrimental impact on the other segments' positions.

Reservations

Apart from the reservations already mentioned above, there are a number of general observations that need to be made that restrict the usefulness of the segment data:

1. The breakdown into three segments is purely arbitrary, and may not reflect a more detailed analysis of smaller segments
2. A detailed analysis of expenditure is required to discover why overall profit has changed
3. An analysis of assets and liabilities needs to be broken down into current and non-current sections so that a proper analysis of liquidity can be made
4. A detailed analysis of finance costs and cash flows would also help identify issues.

Appendix

	Europe		America		Africa	
	2003	**2002**	**2003**	**2002**	**2003**	**2002**
Return on net assets	$\dfrac{70}{(610-260)}$	$\dfrac{69}{(560-240)}$	$\dfrac{90}{(610-250)}$	$\dfrac{90}{(560-230)}$	$\dfrac{(20)}{(300-100)}$	$\dfrac{(40)}{(270-90)}$
	$= 20\%$	$= 21.6\%$	$= 25.0\%$	$= 27.3\%$	$= (10.0\%)$	$= (22.2\%)$
Profit margin	$\dfrac{70}{720}$	$\dfrac{69}{685}$	$\dfrac{90}{610}$	$\dfrac{90}{560}$	$\dfrac{(20)}{440}$	$\dfrac{(40)}{205}$
	$= 9.7\%$	$= 10.1\%$	$= 14.8\%$	$= 16.1\%$	$= (4.5\%)$	$= (19.5\%)$
Asset turnover	$\dfrac{720}{350}$	$\dfrac{685}{320}$	$\dfrac{610}{360}$	$\dfrac{560}{330}$	$\dfrac{440}{200}$	$\dfrac{205}{180}$
	$= 2.10$	$= 2.10$	$= 1.70$	$= 1.70$	$= 2.20$	$= 1.14$
Acid test ratio	$\dfrac{610}{260}$	$\dfrac{560}{240}$	$\dfrac{610}{250}$	$\dfrac{560}{230}$	$\dfrac{300}{100}$	$\dfrac{270}{90}$
	$= 2.35$	$= 2.33$	$= 2.44$	$= 2.43$	$= 3.0$	$= 3.0$
Profitability of associates	$\dfrac{10}{55}$	$\dfrac{9}{52}$	$\dfrac{12}{36}$	$\dfrac{5}{30}$		
	$= 18.2\%$	$= 17.3\%$	$= 33.3\%$	$= 16.7\%$		

Solution 10.3: Diversity

(a) The main items of information required to be disclosed under IAS 14

Companies must identify a 'primary' reporting format (either by product/activity or by geographical area) for its segments. This is normally based on the same format that the company adopts for its own internal management structure. The required items of information for the primary reporting format (for each reportable segment) are:

- sales revenue (split between internal and external sales);
- segment results;
- book value of segmental assets;
- segmental liabilities;
- depreciation and amortisation for the year;
- significant non-cash expenses;
- exceptional items and (via IAS 7) segmental cash flows;
- aggregate of any equity accounted investments (associates/joint ventures) substantially operating within a single segment.

For secondary reporting segments less information is required – mainly segment revenue, total assets and additions to non-current operating assets.

Geographical analysis *re* origin of sales and destination is also required.

(b)   Segmental information and reporting

(i)   *The necessity and benefits of segmental information*

1. Growth of diversified multinational business requires a disaggregation of consolidated data to determine how each part of the business is performing. The parts may be conducting operations in different markets and in different products.
2. Consolidated data may conceal a wide range of profitabilities, contributions to cash flows, risk potentials etc.
3. Segment data are required for analysts to predict the future prospects of the overall business.
4. Comparison of profit margins by themselves would be insufficient – the asset base is necessary as well in order to calculate segment ROCEs.

(ii)   *Problem areas with segmental reporting*

1. There may be difficulties in defining what a reportable segment should be. It is obviously very subjective, and should be changed if a more appropriate analysis is provided.
2. It is the discretion open to directors to decide what their segments are that could potentially hide important information within a segment.
3. There are problems in apportioning common costs – e.g. head office expenses. This should only be carried out if done on a reasonable basis. It will lead to inconsistencies across reporting entities, as some apportion and others do not.
4. Interest costs pose similar problems. Often they are regarded as common costs of financing, but if specific to a segment they should be allocated across the segments concerned.
5. There is a problem with the definition of net assets. If interest is included, then so should finance be included in segment liabilities.

6. There are problems of confidentiality in disclosing too much information about sensitive segments.

(c)   Segmental report for Diversity to 31 March 2000

	Engineering $ million	Chemicals $ million	Supermarkets $ million	Elimination $ million	Consol $ million
Revenue					
External sales	400	300	200		
Inter-segment sales	20	40	nil	(60)	
Total sales	420	340	200	(60)	900
Segmental result (*W1*)	45	79	25		149
Unallocated costs					
Central administration expenses					(37)
Interest (10% on debentures of 120)					(12)
Profit before tax					100
Other information					
Segment/consolidated assets (*W2*)	328	282	130		740
Segment liabilities (*W2*)	(140)	(120)	(30)		(290)
Unallocated corporate liabilities					(120)
Consolidated total liabilities					(410)
Amortisation of goodwill	(6)	(14)			

There is no information *re* other disclosures required by IAS 14 (revised), as the information is not provided in the question.

Working

W1   Segmental profit

	Engineering		Chemicals		Supermarkets	
Cost of sales	(80% × 400)	320	(60% × 300)	180	(75% × 200)	150
Inter-segment cost of sales		20	(60% × 40)	24		nil
Distribution and administration		24		38		25
Goodwill	(allocated 30%)	6	(70%)	14		nil
Interest on finance lease	(50%)	5	(50%)	5		nil
		375		261		175
Total sales		420		340		200
Segmental profit		45		79		25

W2   Segment assets and liabilities

Segment assets

	Engineering		Chemicals		Supermarkets	
Goodwill	(30% × 60)	18	(70% × 60)	42		nil
Owned fixed assets		150		120		100

Leased assets	(60% × 150)	90	(40% ×150)	60	nil
Current assets		70		60	30
		328		282	130
Segment liabilities					
Current liabilities		(40)		(20)	(30)
Lease obligations	(50% × 200)	(100)	(50% × 200)	(100)	nil
		(140)		(120)	(30)

Part of the interest cost (i.e. on finance leases) to those segments that have the finance lease obligations should be allocated. However, debenture costs cannot be specifically allocated. IAS 14 normally expects all interest costs to be treated consistently; thus either they should all be allocated, or none at all. Obviously the same approach would be applied to their related obligations.

Goodwill would normally be carried as a common asset and cost, but in this case the goodwill relates solely to the engineering and chemicals segments of the reporting entity.

11

Employee benefits, pension schemes and share-based payment – solutions

Solution 11.1: Klondike

(a) Relevant features and required accounting treatment of defined contribution and defined benefit schemes

Defined contribution schemes

These schemes define the contributions which employers/employees are prepared to invest in a pension scheme portfolio. The fund is usually managed by a third party. If the funds do not perform, then the employee/pensioner loses. There is no legal requirement for an employer to make good any shortfalls in pension expectations. Thus, from an employer's perspective, the accounting treatment is simple. Whatever contributions are payable, those represent a fair charge against income as the risks lie solely with the employee, not the employer.

Defined benefit schemes

These are often known as final salary schemes, as the pension is promised by the employer to the employee based on years of service and on the final salary at date of retirement. They are 'open ended' in that the risk is always with the employer to make good any short-fall in pension provision. The majority of defined benefit schemes are funded – i.e. the employer makes cash contributions to a separate fund. The employer makes contributions to a fund to build up assets sufficient to meet its contractual obligations. The main problem is the uncertainty that surrounds the future, particularly the total liabilities that will eventually have to be paid out. They will be determined by inflation rates, salary increases, life expectancy, labour turnover rates etc. These assumptions need to be examined and reassessed regularly by actuaries who advise employers as to the appropriate funding to make. Ideally assets in the fund should match the expected liabilities, but even the asset values can change dramatically – as the recent slump in the stock market has shown.

As it will be rare for pension fund assets to match the expected liabilities, a deficit/shortfall will regularly emerge. In the case of a deficit the employer should increase the contributions payable, and in the case of a surplus then a contribution holiday or perhaps a refund could occur.

The accounting treatment is much more complicated for defined benefit schemes. The cost of providing pensions should be charged to the accounting periods in which the benefits are earned by the employees.

Where an actuarial gain or loss arises (caused by actual events differing from forecast events), IAS 19 requires a 10% corridor test to be made. If the gain/loss is within 10% of the greater of the plan's assets or liabilities then the gain or loss may be recognised in the income statement, but it is not required to be. When the gain/loss exceeds the 10% corridor, then the excess has to be recognised in the income statement over the average expected remaining service lives of the employees. This should result in the removal of any large variations in reported profits due to changes in actuarial assumptions.

As a result, the following items should be recognised in income:

- current service cost (i.e. increase in the plan's liability due to the current years service from employees);
- interest cost (i.e. an imputed cost caused by the unwinding of the discount);
- expected return on plan assets (i.e. increase in the market value of the plan's assets);
- actuarial gains and losses recognised under the 10% corridor rule;
- costs of settlements or curtailments.

(b)   Extracts of financial statements

Income statement (extracts)

	$000
Current service costs	160
Interest cost (10% × 1,500)	150
Expected return on assets (12% × 1,500)	(180)
Recognised actuarial gain (*W3*)	(5)
Post retirement cost	125

Balance sheet (extracts)

	$000
Present value of obligations	1,750
Fair value of plan's assets	(1,650)
	100
Unrecognised actuarial gains (*W1*)	140
Liability recognised in balance sheet	240

Working

W1   Unrecognised actuarial gains

Unrecognised actuarial gain at 1 April 2001	200
Actuarial gain on plan assets (*W2*)	10
Actuarial loss on plan liability (*W2*)	(65)
Gain recognised (*W3*)	(5)
	140

W2   *Movement in plan assets and plan liabilities*

	Plan assets $000	Plan liabilities $000
Balance at 1 April 2001	1,500	1,500
Current service costs		160
Interest (1,500 × 10%)		150
Expected return (1,500 × 12%)	180	
Contributions paid	85	
Benefits paid to employees	(125)	(125)
Actuarial gain (bal. fig.)	10	
Actuarial loss (bal. fig.)		65
	1,650	1,750

W3   *Calculation of excess surplus on defined benefit scheme*

Net cumulative unrecognised actuarial gains at 1 April 2001	200
10% corridor (1,500 × 10%)	150
Excess	50

$50,000/10 years = $5,000 actuarial gain to be recognised.

Solution 11.2: A

(a)   Four key issues in the determination of the method of accounting for retirement benefits *re* defined benefit plans

Defined benefit schemes are open ended liabilities for employers. Some of the key issues facing employers in accounting for these schemes are:

1. The determination of the expense – the need to establish a method for recognising and measuring employee benefits. Under IASs, an accruals basis must be adopted rather than cash.
2. The valuation of defined benefit assets – should they be market values?
3. The measurement of plan liabilities – scheme liabilities need to be valued using an actuarial approach. There are two alternative valuation methods: the accrued benefits and prospective benefit approaches.
4. The frequency of actuarial valuations – these are expensive, but should be carried out annually or triennially.
5. The recognition of actuarial gains and losses – whether these should be over the employees' remaining service lives or immediately on the balance sheet. The problem is the volatility created on actuarial gains and losses.
6. Plan amendments – the decision to improve benefits requires thought as to how the cost should be recognised in performance.
7. The nature of the discount rate adopted.

(b)   How IAS 19 deals with the issues

IAS 19 *Employee Benefits* focuses on current values and is on a balance sheet perspective. The surplus/deficit in the fund is to be determined annually, with assets being measured at fair value at the balance sheet. Scheme liabilities should be measured on an actuarial basis using the projected unit basis and a corporate bond to discount the obligations. The net amount appears in the employer's balance sheet as an asset or liability.

Under IAS 19, full actuarial valuations should occur with sufficient regularity such that financial statements do not differ materially from amounts that would be determined at the balance sheet date. The balance sheet asset cannot exceed the net total of:

- unrecognised actuarial losses and past service costs; and
- the present value of any available refunds from the plan or reduction in future contributions to the plan.

Gains and losses measured at the year end are reflected in subsequent years. The amortisation of the net gain/loss is required if it is in excess of 10% of the greater of the defined benefit obligation or the fair value of the plan assets. The period of amortisation cannot exceed the average remaining service period.

IAS 19 provides a choice of possibilities of how to deal with the amount of profit/loss not recognised in the income statement. The actuarial gains/losses can be deferred if the cumulative amount remains inside the 10% corridor. Any amount outside the corridor can be amortised over a shorter period than the working lives of employees, or even immediately, so long as the approach adopted is consistent.

(c) Calculation of the amount that will be shown as the net plan asset in the balance sheet of A as at 31 May 2001

Balance sheet (extracts)

	$m
Present value of obligations	2,000
Fair value of plan's assets	(2,950)
Net surplus	950
Unrecognised actuarial gains (*W1*)	(692)
Asset recognised in balance sheet	258

Income statement (extracts)

	$m
Current service cost	70
Past service cost	25
Interest on liabilities	230
Actuarial gain recognised (*W2*)	(5)
Return on scheme assets	(295)
Net charge to income statement	(25)

Movement in plan surplus

Opening surplus (1,970 assets − 1,500 liabilities)	470
Unrecognised actuarial gain	(247)
Opening net surplus	223
Net charge to income statement	(25)

Contributions paid	60
Closing surplus (2,950 assets − 2,000	
liabilities − unrecognised actuarial gains 692)	258

Working

W1   Unrecognised actuarial gains

Unrecognised actuarial gain at 1 June 2000	247
Actuarial loss on plan liabilities (2,000 − 1,500)	(500)
Actuarial gain on plan assets (2,950 − 1,970)	980
Net contributions in the year (60 − 25 − 5)	(30)
Gain recognised (*W2*)	(5)
Unrecognised actuarial gain at 31 May 2001	692

W2   Calculation of excess surplus on defined benefit scheme

Net cumulative unrecognised actuarial gains at 1 June 2000	247
10% corridor (1,500 × 10% or 10% × £1,970)	(197)
Excess	50

$50,000/10$ years $= \$5,000$ actuarial gain to be recognised.

Solution 11.3: G

(a)   Income statement for the year ended 31 December 2000

	$m	$m
Revenue		1,000
Cost of sales (240 − 5 addit. lump sum + 2 addit. charge)		237
Gross profit		763
Distribution costs (100 + 8 bad debt)	108	
Administration expenses	130	
		238
Profit from operations		525
Interest payable		95
Profit before tax		430
Income tax (120 − 10 over-provision + 80 deferred tax)		190
Profit on ordinary activities after taxation		240
Dividends paid		40
Net profit for the period		200

Balance sheet as at 31 December 2000

	$m	$m
Non-current assets		
Property, plant and equipment		2,400
Goodwill		1,900
		4,300

Current assets

Inventory	110	
Trade and other receivables (90 − 8 bad debt)	82	
Prepayments (pension 5 paid − 2 charged deficit)	3	
Bank	10	
		205

Total assets		4,505
Equity and liabilities		
Issued share capital		500
Share premium		400
Accumulated profits (1,875 + 200 net profit)		2,075
		2,975

Non-current liabilities		
Interest bearing borrowings	1,100	
Deferred tax (200 + 80 charge)	280	
		1,380

Current liabilities		
Trade and other payables	30	
Taxation	120	
		150
		4,505

Notes to the accounts

1. *Taxation*

Current tax charge for the year	120
Over provision of current tax in previous years	(10)
Increase in provision for deferred tax	80
	190

2. *Dividends*

The company has proposed a final dividend of $60m. This is a contingent liability, and should be disclosed in the notes to the financial statements.

3. *Pensions*

The company operates a final pay defined benefit pension scheme. The assets of the scheme are held separately from those of the company. Under IAS 19, unless the surplus/deficit is more than 10% no spreading of that deficit/surplus should be undertaken. However, the directors have decided to spread the deficit of $20m over the average remaining lifetime of employees in the pension scheme.

	$m
Regular pension cost	8
Variation from regular cost ($20/10 years)	2
Net pension cost	10

The $3m prepaid pension cost is not recoverable within 1 year.

4. *Share capital and premium*

	Share capital	**Share premium**	
	$m	**$m**	
Balance at 31 December 1999	400	360	bal. fig.
Issued during the year	100	40	
Balance at 31 December 2000	500	400	

5. *Post-balance sheet event – IAS 10* (Non-adjusting event – to be disclosed in the notes)
A claim for damages of $2m was lodged by a member of the public against the company, after the year end, for serious injury. The matter has now been placed in the hands of the company's solicitors, who are of the opinion that this amount will have to be paid in compensation. The amount is considered material by the directors.

(b) Earnings per share (in accordance with IAS 33)

Earnings	**$m**
Earnings after taxation	240

Capital structure
Shares prior to full issue 400 × 2/12 = 67
Shares post-full issue   500 × 10/12 = 417
                                                484

Earnings per share = $(240m/484m) × 100 = 49.6 c.

(c) Why is such detailed guidance for EPS necessary?

EPS is recognised by many analysts as the 'key' measure of a company's performance, as it encapsulates the overall performance for the year. That can then be compared with previous years, as well as to other companies in the industrial sector. Because it is a relative figure rather than absolute performance, it can relate the monies invested by shareholders to their actual return and let ordinary shareholders have a perspective on how that investment has been performing as opposed to alternative investments, not just in the equities market but also in bonds and property.
    There are many possible variations in how to calculate EPS – whether it should include only ongoing activities, exclude amortisation and depreciation etc. There is a need therefore to find a common method of calculating the ratio and, in particular, to find a common solution across the world so that cross-border listings are made comparable with domestic entities.

(d) What is diluted EPS and why should it be disclosed?

Many companies issue financial instruments which at present do not qualify as ordinary shares but have the ability to do so in the future. If they exercise their powers they will have the effect of spreading the income 'cake' over a greater number of shareholders, and thus it is important for existing shareholders to find out precisely how much worse off they will be when those options are exercised.

There are three main types of diluted securities: convertible preference shares, convertible loans, and share options. In order to find out how much worse off the existing ordinary shareholders will be, the basic earnings are adjusted for the saving in preference dividend and net of tax interest on the former two, as these will no longer have to be paid. The basic capital structure will be adjusted by the number of ordinary shares that convertible loans/shares will be entitled to based on the highest number that they could get their hands on. For options the calculation is a little different, as they will be bringing in cash resources up to the amount of the exercise price so the only dilutable effect is the fact that the exercise price is below the current quoted price. That difference and that percentage of the total shares only should be recorded on the bottom line.

Example – options

Exercise price	$4
Market price	$5
Number of options	1m
Number to be recorded on bottom line for diluted EPS	
1m × 1/5 = 200,000	

There is no adjustment to the top line, as no interest/dividends are currently been paid to the holders of options.

Solution 11.4: SNOB

Note explaining the issues raised

To: Manager
From: Assistant Management Accountant
Date: 14 January 2005

Accounting issues emerging from recent seminar attended by yourself in Rome

(i)   Issue (a) Share-based payment

The practice of issuing share options in exchange for goods and services has become particularly popular over the last few years, particularly in the high tech and start-up situations, where companies need to attract high-quality graduates but cannot afford to pay them large salaries so they offer them a 'piece of the action' as the company takes off. Where goods and services are paid for in cash, the double entry is to credit bank and debit income. The IASB has taken the view that share options are a form of employee remuneration and are part of the 'true' cost of employing staff, and therefore they should be matched against the revenue that they generate from the goods and services generated by those employees. It is a profit and loss approach rather than a balance sheet approach to setting standards, which actually goes against the IASB's own Framework. The standard, **IFRS** 2 *Share-Based Payment*, published in March 2004, does not worry about whether or not the options are actually realised, and thus the value of the options remains permanently on the balance sheet and is not removed.

The most common form of share-based payment is to reward employees for services undertaken, although it is also equally applied to suppliers if they are paid in that form. The principle upon which the accounting treatment is based is that employees have provided services which, were they settled in cash, would certainly result in a charge to income, and therefore a fair presentation can only be achieved if a similar charge is made for share-based payments.

The biggest problem is deciding the charge to be made to income. First, it should be a fair value which could be measured either by reference to market prices of quoted securities or, if unquoted, by reference to an appropriate option pricing model. These values would be regarded as surrogates for the fair value of goods and services generated by the employees, which would be very difficult to measure. A second issue is the date that the fair value should be measured. If the share-based payment is to be settled by equity, that fair value should always be based at the date of the original grant of the options and the actual charge to income ultimately must be based on the actual number of employees who have achieved their targets and are therefore entitled to exercise their rights. For cash settled transactions, ultimately it will be the intrinsic value of the shares at the date of exercise, but if not exercised it will be based on their fair value each year until the date of expiry, when a transfer may be made from debt to reserves as these are treated as liabilities initially.

As our own share-based payment agreements are share appreciation rights, we will initially have to debit income and credit liabilities with the fair value of the options using the Black Scholes Model and then subsequently adjust to intrinsic value when they are exercised, and finally transfer any unexercised options after the expiry date from debt into reserves.

(ii)   Issue (b) Non-financial disclosures

Financial reports are only part of the overall information provided to users when seeking to acquire useful information about an enterprise. These traditionally have tended to look backwards and to focus on the needs of one particular user group – the equity investor. Effectively, other users such as creditors, the public and government need to look beyond the annual report to meet their specific needs.

However, it has now become acceptable to introduce more social and environmental reporting inside the Annual Report. That has been encouraged by professional bodies, and often companies have tended in the past to provide a separate social and environmental report. The advantage of publishing these reports is that it can improve the quality of information available to the workforce, which can engender a contented workforce and a contented local community who might otherwise be concerned about the impact that the company has on its local environment. There is also increasing stringent environmental legislation being introduced, which is beginning to result in major fines being paid for not having environment-friendly policies. In Europe new polluter licences are being awarded to manufacturing industries which will be tradable in the open market, so it is better to be ahead of the game and disclose current policies in the annual report so that no surprises are around the corner.

Social and environment disclosure is voluntary at present, but it is very likely that it will become compulsory in the future. Such disclosure is already perceived to be best practice in large and listed corporations, and it is very likely that this could be extended to companies of a similar size to ours. It would therefore be advisable to consider seriously our overall social and environment policies and begin to record some of these policies within the annual report.

(iii)   Issue (c) Off balance sheet finance

Off balance sheet finance (OBSF) is a term used to refer to any situation where an entity has deliberately entered into a transaction that results in a financial obligation not being displayed on the balance sheet as a liability. There have been hundreds of these schemes developed over the years, and clearly there is a danger that the full impact of a company's borrowings may not be reflected on the balance sheet. Entities may wish to leave such finance off balance sheet for the following reasons:

- a high level of borrowings is seen by many users as indicative of financial instability and leads to very high gearing ratios being presented;
- the entity may have legal covenants regarding their permitted level of borrowings that could be breached if these OBSF obligations were to be reported on balance sheet;
- the recognition of a borrowing on balance sheet is always associated with a related asset, otherwise the double entry would not be complied with. Increased asset values lead to increased capital employed, which can reduce key performance ratios.

Unlike in the UK/Ireland, there is no international accounting standard that specifically covers OBSF, although finance leases must be capitalised under IAS 17 *Leases*. However, *The Framework for the Preparation and Presentation of Financial Statements* has, as a basic principle, the notion that transactions should be accounted for in accordance with their economic substance rather than their legal form.

It is likely that, at some stage in the future, the IASB will develop an international financial reporting standard that will abolish the distinction between finance and operating leases. This is because the leasing industry has attempted deliberately to ensure that as many leases as possible be classified as operating and thus kept off balance sheet. Thus a fair presentation of the financial statements has not been possible. That may be the start of a more comprehensive international standard on the subject. However, to date the ASB is the only standard setter that has set a general substance standard – FRS 5 *Reporting the Substance of Transactions*.

The impact on ourselves in the immediate future will be the on operating leases that we hold on some of our properties. Undoubtedly these will, in the next few years, be reclassified as finance, and this could have damaging impact on our current gearing ratios. This will need to be carefully investigated over the next two years.

12

Financial instruments – solutions

Solution 12.1:

(a)   The strengths and weaknesses of historical cost accounting

The main strengths of adopting historic costs are as follows:

- it is easy to understand;
- it is objective as the original costs are usually factual;
- it can be reliably measured;
- it has been used since accounting began, so users are familiar with it.

The main weaknesses, however, are that:

- for non-current assets, historic cost bears no relation to their actual value;
- depreciation is inadequate to replace the asset;
- holding gains are included in profit whereas they are needed to maintain the existing operating capacity of the business;
- assets which have no original cost are ignored (e.g. homegrown brands).

(b)   Why current value is more appropriate for financial instruments

Financial instruments have always been very volatile in terms of their valuation. They vary as the stock market, interest rates and exchange rates change; thus to keep them at their historic cost would not reveal their true worth – which is important, as they can crystallise very quickly into real assets or liabilities. Only by keeping the values up to date can users have any confidence in their overall worth.

Financial instruments can often have no initial cost as their value derives from an underlying financial instrument, so if they were to be recorded at cost they would not appear at all on the balance sheet. In that case it is essential to fair value the instruments so that users have a better idea of what impact they would have on the business if they were to crystallise.

(c)   Why were the disclosure requirements of IAS 32 inadequate?

IAS 32 *Financial Instruments: Presentation and Disclosure* was published to improve the notes to the accounts with regard to financial instruments, but it did not impact on the balance sheet itself. Readers rarely look at the notes, and they expect the balance sheet to reveal a fair presentation without having to delve into quite complicated notes. Also, IAS 32 did not bring any rules as to how to measure financial instruments at fair value, so the risks attached to many instruments might not necessarily be picked up by the reader.

IAS 32 did try to alter the presentation of financial instruments by insisting on them being recorded according to their substance. In that regard, redeemable preference shares are now classified as debt and convertible loans are split, being their equity and their debt elements on the balance sheet.

IAS 32 is now backed up by IAS 39 *Financial Instruments: Recognition and Measurement*, which forces reporting entities to fair value many of their financial instruments and to record these values on the balance sheet, as well as revealing any gains/losses thereon within the income statement for the year and not in reserves.

(d) The likely impact of international accounting practice of IAS 39

The implementation of fair value reporting is a political hot potato. It has reached the highest level of politics, with the French president, Jacques Chirac, putting his weight against the adoption of IAS 39 in its full entirety into European accounting practice. In this he is abetted by the large French banks, particularly Credit Lyonnais, which are very concerned about the impact of increased volatility in the banks' performance statements. They believe it will lead to the need to retain more resources in the business to combat that volatility, and thus less resources to be lent out to their customers. It is argued that this could have a serious detrimental impact on the French economy. As a result, the EU has decided to 'carve out' large parts of IAS 39 from being implemented in January 2005.

Solution 12.2: Tall

(a) What are the problems in the way that financial instruments have been accounted for in the past that have led to the issuance of these standards?

Financial instruments, and particularly derivatives, have always posed problems for both investors and accountants to understand. The Nick Leeson affair, resulting in the ultimate collapse of Barings Bank in London, is one of many scandals pertinent to the issue.

The newer financial instruments have the ability to transform the risk profile of a reporting entity in a way that was never foreseen a few years ago. A derivative, for example, can be acquired for zero cost and thus not recorded on the balance sheet. However, it can be used to convert a floating rate liability of one currency into a fixed rate liability of another, or to hedge the fact that future sales may be worth less in a year's time as the local currency might strengthen in the meantime.

The value of a derivative, therefore, can change significantly from day to day and year to year. Unfortunately, under the historical cost system these potential large gains and losses are not reported until they realise and by that stage it is too late to save the company.

The system also leads unscrupulous accountants to 'cherry pick' and manoeuvre unrealised gains into bad years and *vice versa*.

IAS 32 has been brought in mainly to ensure that the substance of these financial instrument transactions is presented on the balance sheet and proper disclosure provided. IAS 39 goes further and details how to apply the fair value model to both measuring and recognising these financial instruments on the balance sheet.

(b)   Memorandum to assistant *re* Tall

To: Assistant Management Accountant
From: Management Accountant
Date: 20 January 2005
Subject: Accounting treatment of new funding arrangements

Presentation of financial instruments

You have expressed the opinion that both the new 15m $1 bonds and the 10m $1 preferred shares should be classified as equity on the balance sheet on the grounds that legally the preferred shares are in fact shares, and because it is likely that the bondholders will elect to convert their bonds into equity in 5 years' time and they therefore have similar characteristics to the preferred shares.

Unfortunately your recommendation is not in line with IAS 32, which governs both the presentation and the disclosure of financial instruments. Under IAS 32, a distinction is made between those instruments which are equity and those which are debt. As the company has a legal obligation to redeem the bonds on maturity they must be treated as debt, but they also have to take into account the equity element. Thus IAS 32 requires us to adopt 'split accounting' by breaking up the instrument into its debt and equity components separately and thus reflecting the substance of the arrangement.

The preference shares, if non-redeemable, could be treated as equity, but there is a clear redemption date and the company cannot avoid paying back the principal at that time. They should therefore be classified as debt, and not equity, on the balance sheet.

(i)   Computation of the finance cost

I understand that you have no idea of how to deal with the associated finance costs involved with the two instruments as regards treatment in the income statement.

The measurement of financial instruments is governed by IAS 39. Under that standard, most instruments must be fair valued – i.e. marked to market.

The bonds and preferred shares will therefore carry the following finance costs:

- the amounts paid to the holders via interest and/or dividends; and
- the increase or decrease in the fair value between the start and end of the year.

In both cases the full charge will be recorded within 'finance costs' – the preference charge is therefore regarded as a 'true' expense rather than the current legal appropriation of profit treatment.

(ii)   *Possible adoption of uniting of interests method of consolidation*

The original accounting standard, IAS 22 *Business Combinations*, only permitted the adoption of uniting of interests consolidation (i.e. merger accounting) in very rare circumstances. However, due to particular problems emerging in the United States and the fact that they abolished uniting of interests or pooling in August 2001, the rest of the world has had to follow suit. All the major standard setters, bar the ASB in Great Britain and Ireland, have followed the US pattern and abolished the model. The IASB published their updated standard in March 2004 with the same title as IAS 22, and have agreed to follow the US line and also abolish the technique.

Effectively it now means that regardless of the source of funding for a business combination it will have to be consolidated through the purchase or acquisition method. An acquirer will need to be identified and a fair value exercise will have to be undertaken in all circumstances. Goodwill will be created as a residual but also as a permanent asset that will have to be reviewed for impairment on an annual basis. There will be scope to bring in 'other intangibles' instead of classifying the residual as goodwill, as long as these can be reliably measured and there is a probability of benefits flowing from them. Expectations are that a number of very unusual 'new' intangible assets will emerge, to include trade dress, customer lists, secret recipes etc. These can still be amortised over their estimated useful lives, and this might considerably reduce the impact of goodwill impairment.

13

Sundry financial reporting standards – solutions

Solution 13.1: The Lucky Dairy

Advice to directors

IAS 41 *Agriculture* prescribes the accounting treatment, presentation and disclosures related to agricultural activity. A biological asset such as a dairy herd should be measured at each balance sheet date at its fair value less estimated point of sale costs, except where the fair value cannot be measured reliably. The fair value of cattle is the price in the relevant market less the transport and other costs of getting the cattle to that market. Any gains or losses arising from a change in fair value should be included in net profit or loss for the period in which it arises. IAS 41 encourages companies to separate the change in fair value less estimated point of sale costs between that due to physical changes and the portion attributable to price changes. The calculations are in the Appendix. The company is encouraged by IAS 41 to provide a quantified description of each group of biological assets. Thus the cows and heifers should be shown and quantified separately in the balance sheet.

Milk should be valued under IAS 41 at its fair value at the time of milking less estimated point of sale costs. However, due to the bad publicity the inventory of milk has risen tenfold from 50,000 kilograms to 500,000 kilograms. There is a need to ascertain whether the milk is fit for consumption and whether there will be a need to dispose of some of it. The quantity of milk which will not be sold should be determined and written off the value of the inventory. This amount should be disclosed separately in the income statement under IAS 8 *Accounting Policies, Changes in Accounting Estimates and Errors* as it has arisen due to the disease in the cattle.

Unconditional government grants should be recognised as income under IAS 41 when and only when the government grant becomes receivable. Although there had been a statement on 1 April 2002 that the grant was to be paid, it was only on 6 June 2002 that an official letter was received stating the amount to be paid to Lucky, and therefore the $1.5m should be recognised as income in the year to 31 May 2003.

IAS 37 *Provisions, Contingent Liabilities and Contingent Assets* indicates that where there is a present obligation as a result of a past event which will probably result in an outflow of resources, then a provision should be recognised for the best estimate to settle the obligation. In this case the lawyers have indicated that it is probable that Lucky will become liable for the illness of consumers of the milk, and that therefore a provision for $2m should be made.

IAS 37 is quite specific on expected reimbursement of costs. Such reimbursement should only be recognised when it is virtually certain that it will be received. In this case the reimbursement is only 'possible', and therefore an asset will not be recognised for the compensation which may be paid by the government. However, the expected reimbursement will be disclosed in the financial statements, stating that there has been no asset recognised for that expected compensation payment.

Given the various events that have affected the company during the period, it would seem that consideration should be given to the impairment of the herd's value in the Dale region as it is the only one affected by the disease. The Dale region can be identified as a separate cash generating unit (CGU), and where a biological asset's fair value is not reliable it should be valued at cost less any impairment losses. In the Appendix this value is shown at $1.2m.

IAS 35 *Discontinuing Operations* is operational once an 'initial disclosure event' has occurred. Under the IAS, this is deemed to be the earlier of when the company entered into a binding sale agreement or when the directors have approved the detailed plan for the discontinuance and announced it. In the case of the Dale region, although it has approved the plan it has not been announced officially, although a newspaper has published an article on the possible discontinuance. A constructive obligation has to have been created, and for this to be a valid expectation that the Dale region farms will be sold must also have been created. The Dale region satisfies the criteria of IAS 35 whereby the component of the company being sold must be distinguishable for operational and financial purposes. However, because there has not yet been a public announcement the company may change its mind, and, although the newspaper article may have alerted the public, it does not necessarily create a 'constructive obligation'. The new standard, IFRS 5 *Non Current Assets Held for Sale and Presentation of Discontinued Operations* does not alter that treatment.

Appendix

Valuation of cattle stock excluding the Dale region

			$000	$000
Fair value as at 1 June 2001	(50,000 × $50)			2,500
Purchase of cattle as at 1 December		(25,000 × $40)		1,000
Increase in fair value due to price changes				
	(50,000 × ($55 − 50))		250	
	(25,000 × ($42 − 40))		50	
				300
Increase in fair value due to physical changes				
	(50,000 × ($60 − 55))		250	
	(25,000 × ($46 − 42))		100	
				350
Fair value as at 31st May 2002				
	(50,000 × $60)		3,000	
	(25,000 × $46)		1,150	
				4,150

Valuation of cattle in Dale region

The above table shows the valuation of all cattle, excluding the Dale region, assuming that fair value can be established. However, in the Dale region it was felt that the fair value could not be reliably measured on initial recognition. Therefore, the cattle and heifers should be measured at cost less any impairment losses until the fair value of the asset becomes measurable. It is considered that this is not yet the case with these animals.

	$000
20,000 cows at cost ($50) at 1 June 2001	1,000
10,000 heifers at cost ($40) at 1 June 2001	400
	1,400
Net selling price	1,000
Value in use (discounted value of milk)	1,200

The value of cows is impaired and should be valued at the value in use of $1,200,000.

The value of the herd at 31 May 2002 in the Dale region would have been 20,000 cows at $60 + 10,000 heifers at $55, i.e. $1.75m, but for the unreliability of the herd's fair value.